796.357 Durant, John
DUR

    Baseball's miracle
    teams

DATE DUE			
209 DEC 9			
183 DEC 10			
OCT 9 89 210			
OCT 23 89 210			
OCT 1 '91 203			
211			

GAYLORD 234   PRINTED IN U. S. A.

© THE BAKER & TAYLOR CO.

Baseball's Miracle Teams

Baseball's Miracle Teams

By JOHN DURANT

Illustrated with photographs

HASTINGS HOUSE · PUBLISHERS
New York 10016

*To Joan Payson, who brought baseball back
to life in New York and ought to be in the
Cooperstown Hall of Fame.*

LIBRARY OF CONGRESS CATALOGING IN PUBLICATION DATA
Durant, John date   Baseball's miracle teams.

SUMMARY: An account of how three last place teams, the Boston Braves in
1914, the New York Giants in 1951, and the New York Mets in 1969, surprisingly
developed winning streaks and swept their way to first place.
1. New York (City). Baseball club (National League, Mets)—Juvenile literature. 2. New York (City). Baseball club (National League, Giants)—Juvenile
literature. 3. Boston. Baseball club (National League)—Juvenile literature.
[1. New York (City). Baseball club (National League, Mets) 2. New York
(City). Baseball club (National League, Giants) 3. Boston. Baseball club
(National League) 4. Baseball] I. Title.
GV875.N45D78   796.357'64'0973   74-34571
ISBN 0-8038-0765-1

Published simultaneously in Canada by
Saunders of Toronto, Ltd., Don Mills, Ontario

Printed in the United States of America

Contents

AUTHOR'S NOTE

If by some magic a fan could see a baseball game as it was played in 1914, what would it look like to him? He would probably marvel at its similarity to today's game but he would notice that almost everything was on a smaller scale.

The average big leaguer was a couple of inches shorter than the modern athlete. The glove he wore was much smaller, about half the size of the big leather baskets now in use. The ball parks were small and intimate. Fans sat in wooden stands that ran close to the foul lines. They were so near the players they could hear them chatter back and forth on the diamond.

This was before the lively ball was brought into the game and even the top sluggers did not hit many homers. A whole team would hit only about 20 a season.

But they could hit. There were far more 300 hitters then and it was no easier for them to get a hit than it is now. In fact, it may have been more difficult. They swung thick, fat-handled bats and pitchers were allowed to throw the spitball and other trick deliveries which have since been outlawed. Pitchers were as fast as today's breed.

The players ran the bases like wild men. They stole more than three times the number of bases that modern players steal in a season. They were exciting to watch.

Do not think of them as quaint oldtimers in baggy pants playing a different game than we know. They played under the same basic rules that exist today. The size and dimensions of the diamond, the distance between the bases have remained exactly the same to the fraction of an inch. It is the same game. The men who excelled in it years ago would have been stars at any time in the game's long history.

1

The Boston Braves

Up From the Depths

In 1912 the most hopeless team in baseball was the Boston Braves. For 10 years they had finished no higher than sixth place in the eight-club National League. They were dead last five times and next to last three times.

They had six managers in six years but that did not help them any. They kept right on losing. Nothing seemed to work. They set records in errors one season. Their bats were feeble. One year they lost 19 games in a row.

Most humiliating was what pitcher Joe McGinnity of the New York Giants did to the Braves one sunny afternoon in Boston. He pitched a double header and beat them twice, going all the way in both games. They called him "Iron Man" Joe McGinnity.

The Boston fans gave up on the Braves. Their favorite team was the Red Sox of the American League. The Sox were the world champions at that time and Fenway Park, their home grounds, was always crowded when they played.

Across the city, the Braves played to empty seats in their park, the South End Grounds. A bleacher seat in those days

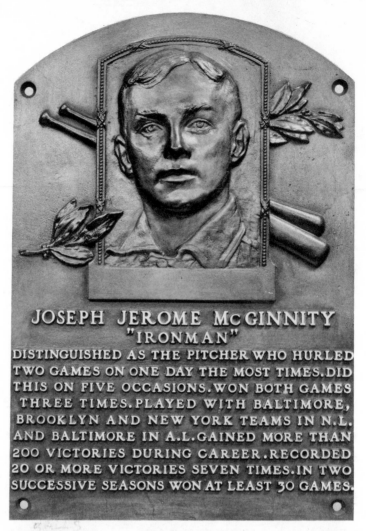

JOSEPH JEROME McGINNITY
"IRONMAN"
DISTINGUISHED AS THE PITCHER WHO HURLED
TWO GAMES ON ONE DAY THE MOST TIMES. DID
THIS ON FIVE OCCASIONS. WON BOTH GAMES
THREE TIMES. PLAYED WITH BALTIMORE,
BROOKLYN AND NEW YORK TEAMS IN N.L.
AND BALTIMORE IN A.L. GAINED MORE THAN
200 VICTORIES DURING CAREER. RECORDED
20 OR MORE VICTORIES SEVEN TIMES. IN TWO
SUCCESSIVE SEASONS WON AT LEAST 30 GAMES.

"Ironman" Joe McGinnity's plaque in baseball's Hall of Fame. He pitched
a doubleheader against the Braves and won both games.

cost only 25 cents, but the fans wouldn't pay even that much
to watch the Braves. They were a miserable team, said the fans
—a joke.

They were no joke to Jim Gaffney, though. He bought the
Braves in 1912 and he suffered all through that season. His club
lost 101 games out of 153 played and finished last for the fourth
straight year.

Gaffney knew that something had to be done to lift the Braves
out of the cellar and put them in the first division. The way
things were going the club might fold up and die. Losing money

was not important to Gaffney. What counted more was his lost pride. He wanted the satisfaction of putting a good team on the field, a fighting, spirited team, one that he could be proud of. That meant a lot more to him than any money he might make or lose as owner of baseball's worst team.

Gaffney knew of a manager who was famous for improving poor teams. He had managed several major-league and minor-league clubs and in every case they had gone uphill under his leadership. His name was George Tweedy Stallings, manager of Buffalo of the International League.

Late in the 1912 season Gaffney and Stallings met in New York and watched the eighth-place Braves take a drubbing from the Giants. As usual, the Braves were weak at the plate and made more than their share of errors.

"Well," said Gaffney, "how do they look to you?"

"Terrible," replied Stallings. "They need lots of changes."

"You're the boss," answered Gaffney. "You make the changes. We've got to have a winner."

"I always seem to get hopeless teams," Stallings said. "But this one is the worst I ever saw." *

Next year at spring training quarters Stallings took over the club. The players eyed him curiously, wondering what sort of a person he was. They soon found out.

George Stallings was a handsome, dark-complexioned man with brown eyes and gleaming white teeth. He was born in Augusta, Georgia, the son of a Confederate General.

He was baseball's strangest man. He had two distinct personalities. Away from the ball park he was a polite, dignified gentleman, elegant in his dress and manners.

On the bench he was another personality. He was triggered-tempered and would fly into a rage at the slightest misplay by one of his men. His tongue lashing were frequent and violent, as his players discovered before the season had hardly begun.

Stallings was overly superstitious. He would never walk under a ladder or let a black cat cross his path. In the dugout he insisted upon having the bats placed in exact order and

* All discussions, monologues, and quoted thoughts in this volume are derived directly from published interviews and newspaper items.

kept that way until the game ended. If the order was changed, the Braves would surely lose, he believed.

One time at lunch before a game George ordered lemon pie for desert. "Maybe the pie will change our luck," he said. The Braves had lost their third game in a row the day before.

Sure enough, that afternoon the Braves won. George ordered lemon pie the next day and again the Braves won. They kept on winning and George kept on eating lemon pie. The winning streak lasted nine days. It was the longest one the Braves had known for many years. And the club moved out of the cellar.

Whenever the Braves began a rally George would stay motionless on the spot no matter where he was sitting or standing, until the batting spree was over. In one game he was sitting on the bench and was bent over tying a shoelace when his catcher, Hank Gowdy, cracked out a double. George froze in his stooped position and remained that way while the next man came to bat. *Wham!* another hit and Gowdy scored. George didn't dare to move a muscle for fear of jinxing the drive. The rally was just beginning. It lasted half an hour, but not until the final out did George try to straighten himself. He couldn't do it and had to be helped to the clubhouse.

He had his favorite seat on the bench. It was his lucky spot and he would sit on it every day. But he could never stay there very long. As the game went on he grew more restless and could not keep still. He'd slide back and forth along the bench. After a few games the seat of his pants were shiny and as thin as paper. He used to wear out a pair of pants almost every other week.

George originated a most unusual sign, which he flashed from the bench when he wanted a runner to steal a base. He would pretend to smile and would display his pearly-white teeth in full. Against his dark skin and the shadows of the dugout his toothy smile glowed like a light bulb. The sign could easily be seen by his coaches or players on base. It never failed. When he really smiled at something he'd cover his mouth with his hand if there were men on the bases.

In spite of Stalling's harsh language and his peculiar superstitions, the players liked their new manager from the start. He was an excellent instructor and knew the game thoroughly. He talked to his players in the clubhouse like a teacher in a classroom. They said he would have made a great college professor.

He inspired them with his spirit and drive, and in his first season as manager brought them up to fifth place. They had not finished that high in more than 10 years.

Still, it was not a pennant. And George was no fifth-place manager. He knew he needed a few new players to cover the weak spots in the lineup.

He already had some talented men. There was Rabbit Maranville, the small shortstop who stood only five feet, five inches; Hank Gowdy, the lanky, red-headed catcher, and Dick Rudolph, who was small for a pitcher but had superb control and a great curve.

In February of 1914 Stallings took his men south for spring training. He lectured them daily and the players listened to every word. He repeatedly told them that this was the year they were going to the top. He was convinced that if they

George Stallings, manager of the 1914 Boston Braves, flashes his famous smile. He gave signals from the bench by exposing his pearly teeth.

believed they could win, they would win. "The team that won't be beat, can't be beat," he insisted.

The players began to believe him. They took pride in themselves. But there were times when they hated him. He drove them hard. He staged long, tiring workouts and made his pitchers run up to four miles a day.

The team he put together that spring was a set of brash, impudent youngsters bursting with life and energy. They were small in stature. Only two or three on the squad reached six feet in height. "A wild bunch of kids," was one reporter's description of them.

A newcomer to the club was Johnny Evers. He had been playing manager of the Chicago Cubs before he came to the Braves in 1914. He had made a name for himself as a scrapper and a leader. Stallings made him team captain. Johnny played second base and weighed only 125 pounds, but he was a fighter all the way.

In spring training he ran his players ragged. If anybody on the team eased up or shirked his duty, Johnny would light into him. He considered it a personal insult. Stallings made an excellent choice when he named Johnny to lead the team on the field.

One big question remained, however, as the team headed north to open the season. It was the nine-man pitching staff. It was centered around three key men who would have to do almost all the pitching that summer. Could they stand the pressure, or would they collapse?

The three stalwarts were Dick Rudolph, Bill James and Lefty Tyler. Dick Rudolph had been a star pitcher at Fordham University in New York. He was given a tryout by the Giants but manager John McGraw turned him down because he didn't think the five-foot, nine-inch Rudolph was big enough to pitch in the majors.

Bill James, whose spitball was the most baffling in the league, stood a towering six feet, three inches and weighed 196 pounds. The now illegal pitch was difficult to hit. The ball, wet with saliva or tobacco juice, would slide off a pitcher's fingers and would not

12

Johnny Evers (right), team captain of the miracle Braves, played second base. He was a fiery competitor and an inspiring leader in every game.

rotate as it wobbled toward the plate. Bill also had a good fastball.

Lefty Tyler, a southpaw, was a power-pitcher with a blazing fastball. He had great stamina and worked superbly under pressure.

Stallings knew that outside of the Big Three he did not have much of a pitching staff. He decided to work Rudolph, James and Tyler every third day. That meant that each man would have only two days of rest between games. The usual practice, then and now, is to give a pitcher at least three days of rest.

Stallings didn't see it that way. "A pitcher's arm is still sore the day after a game," he said, "but he can get a good rest that day. The second day he'll get massages and he'll be ready to pitch again the third day. My pitchers won't crack."

He was criticised by baseball writers who did not like his

13

rotation system. They thought that he was asking too much of his hurlers. And it seemed that way as the season got under way.

The Big Three failed to deliver. The Braves could not get going. They lost 18 of their first 22 games. They looked as bad as ever. Johnny Evers got sick and the Rabbit came down with tonsilitis. The team was dispirited. Out of desperation Stallings made some trades in the hope of improving the club. Still, the Braves kept losing.

Stallings urged his players not to give up hope. "Don't quit; we can do it," he told them. In an interview with the baseball writers, he said: "Give us another month and we'll be leading the league," Stallings said. They thought George had lost his mind. The Braves were in last place.

On July 4, almost the mid-point of the pennant race, they were still floundering in the cellar. They were 15 games behind the leading Giants, and the worst was yet to come.

It came in Buffalo a few days later when the Braves stopped off there to play an exhibition game. No one expected them to lose to Buffalo, a minor league team, but they not only lost—they got their ears pinned back to the tune of 15 to 2. It was bad enough to lose to a National League club, but to get crushed by such a lopsided score by minor leaguers was unforgiveable. This was the ultimate humiliation.

It was almost the breaking point for Stallings. That night in the train as it headed west, he walked through the Braves' car staring at each player. Three times he walked up and down the aisle between the seated players without uttering a word. Then he stopped and stared in disgust at the whole team. "Big Leaguers, huh!" he said, and spat upon the floor.

It was the Buffalo disaster that seemed to start the Braves on their way up. They won the first two games they played on their western trip. They extended their winning streak to nine victories out of 12 games played.

On a Sunday morning on the 19th of July while the Braves were having breakfast in Cincinnati, they were still in last place. But they were now 11 games behind the front-running Giants instead of 15, and only one game in back of seventh-place Pittsburg.

14

That afternoon they played a double-header against the Reds. After winning the first game, the Braves fell behind in the second game and looked like sure losers going into the ninth inning. The Reds were leading, 2-0, when the Braves came to bat for the last time. Stallings was sliding back and forth on the bench in agony. "Get on, get on!" he urged Red Smith, his third baseman, who was at the plate waiting for the first pitch. Red must have heard his boss, for he promptly lashed out a double and made second standing up. It was the start of a rally.

Bang! bang! bang! It sounded like firecrackers going off one after the other as the Braves scattered hits all over the field. When the dust finally settled they were in front 3 to 2, and that was the final score.

The double victory moved them up a notch to seventh place. Down went Pittsburg to the bottom of the league.

Next on the schedule was a critical five-game series with Pittsburg on the Pirates' home grounds. It was there that the Big Three were at their magnificent best. They stunned and overwhelmed the Pirates with their brilliant pitching. At the

On the bench with manager Stallings are the Braves' Big Three pitchers (from left to right): Bill James, George Tyler and Dick Rudolph.

Rabbit Maranville was noted for his pranks on and off the field, but he was the best shortstop of his time. He made the Hall of Fame in 1954.

same time they inspired their teammates. Here is what they did:

Dick Rudolph, the tricky little right-hander, pitched a shutout; then Bill James with his baffling spitter held the Pirates scoreless, and Lefty Tyler subdued them completely for another shutout. As if that wasn't enough, James and Tyler working together pitched the fourth shutout.

The Braves dropped one game, but left town winners of four out of five games. With their spirits soaring they immediately reeled off nine straight victories. They were on fire now; nothing could stop them.

Owner Gaffney was so grateful that he summoned the whole team to his office and thanked them. Then he signed up each man to play for him the next season. No matter what happened, now they were guaranteed jobs for another year, win or lose.

The team was at last enjoying life, and no one enjoyed it more than Rabbit Maranville. As a prankster he had no equal in baseball. He loved to have fun, on and off the field. One time just for laughs he dove fully clothed into a pool of goldfish in a hotel lobby. Stallings did not mind the Rabbit's pranks as long as the team was doing well.

Another time in a game while stealing second, he dove through the outstretched legs of umpire Hank O'Day. The Rabbit avoided the tag and O'Day called him safe. The umpire pulled out his rule book and thumbed through it but he could find no regulation the Rabbit had broken.

Once, when umpire Bob Hart was having an arm-waving argument with Johnny Evers, the Rabbit crept on hands and knees behind Hart. Then standing up, he imitated the umpire's every gesture in pantomine. The fans roared with laughter. The umpire could not understand what was so funny.

While the team was on a western trip in July, the Rabbit played a prank on Stallings that become the talk of the baseball world. Somehow the small shortstop got hold of a bellhop's uniform and put it on. With a telegram in his hand he went to Stalling's hotel room. The manager was in the tub when the Rabbit knocked on the bathroom door. "Telegram for Mr. Stallings," he said through the half-open door and handed him the message. The Rabbit kept his arm extended and turned his face away from Stallings so that he wouldn't be recognized.

"What are you waiting for, boy?" growled Stallings.

"A tip, you cheapskate," yelled the Rabbit, and retreated through the bedroom.

The enraged manager leapt from the tub, hastily draped himself with a towel and chased his laughing shortstop down the corridor.

The impish Rabbit got his nickname because of the way he hopped around the infield and gobbled up grounders. He would catch a pop fly by cupping his hands together high against his chest and letting the ball drop into the pocket he formed. His "vest pocket catches" became his trademark and delighted fans everywhere.

For all his colorful antics on and off the field, he was a fine player. He was, in fact, a great shortstop. He saved many a game for the Braves with his "impossible" stops and his accurate, snap throws to the bases. He had a career batting average of .258 and was admitted to the Baseball Hall of Fame in 1954 mainly because of his superb defensive play.

It was a close, tough pennant race as the Braves headed home from their western trip. The Giants had a comfortable lead in July, but the other seven clubs were bunched together. They were so close to each other that it took the red-hot Braves only three weeks to climb from seventh place to second. And that is where they stayed all during August.

Slowly, however, they began closing the gap between themselves and the Giants. Manager McGraw looked over his shoulder long enough to call the Braves "A gang of misfits." He had won three consecutive pennants and was confident of a fourth. It was unthinkable that the Braves could topple him from the pinnacle.

One wonders, though, what his thoughts were about little Dick Rudolph, the 160-pound pitcher McGraw had let go because he was "too small." Here was Dick in a Braves' uniform setting down the Giants and enjoying every minute of it. He won 27 games for the Braves that year. Had McGraw kept him the pennant would surely have gone to the Giants. They called Dick "McGraw's worst mistake."

At last, the Braves took over first place—on September 2. They dropped to second the next day, then drew even with the Giants just before their big Labor Day series with them.

At that time all of Europe was aflame. World War I had started. Millions of men were fighting and dying throughout Europe. America would soon take part in it.

But around Boston as Labor Day approached, one would hardly know that a terrible war was about to engulf the world. The talk in the streets and in shops and restaurants all over town was not about the German invasion of France. It was about another kind of invasion—of the Giants invading Boston and the great battle that was about to take place for the championship of the National League.

The Braves' South End Grounds was far too small for the crowds that wanted to see this decisive, three-game series. The Red Sox let the Braves use their more spacious Fenway Park. The teams met there on the morning of September 7 before an overflow crowd of 36,000.

McGraw called upon the great Christie Mathewson, his ace of aces, to take the mound for the Giants. Rated by many baseball historians as the finest of all pitchers, Matty was a control artist without equal. Some of his National League records

Christy Mathewson—the master of them all, in the opinion of many experts. His 37 triumphs in one season is still the National League record high.

still stand: pitched 68 consecutive innings without walking a man, 1913; won 37 games, 1908; pitched three shutouts in 1905 World Series.

Matty was held in high esteem around the league. Opposing players rarely "rode," or taunted, him from the bench. Not so, the young and sassy Braves. As the slightly knock-kneed Matty strode toward the mound they shouted insults. "Here comes old Milk Legs," they yelled. "You think you can stop us, Milk Legs? Not a chance."

(The "Milk Legs" slur stemmed from the knock-kneed position a farmer assumes when he sits on a stool with his legs astride the pail as he milks a cow.)

Matty was then in the twilight of his career. He was not as sharp as he had been. Nevertheless, he was in command that morning and kept the Giants in front inning after inning.

When the Giants came to bat in the ninth the score was 4 to 3 in their favor. Dick Rudolph held them in check, and then it was the Braves' turn at the plate.

Matty got his first man on a pop fly, then faced Josh Devore, a speedy outfielder but a weak hitter. He was batting only .227. Josh chopped a slow grounder toward first and just managed to get there ahead of the ball. Next up was tiny Herbie Moran, a five-foot, five-inch outfielder. Only three days before in Philadelphia he had been knocked cold by a beanball. Herbie got hold of a slow curve and drove the ball deep into the outfield. It disappeared into the overflow crowd and was a ground-rule double. Josh was forced to stop at third because of the rule.

Now with men on second and third, one out, and the Braves still trailing, 4-3, up came Johnny Evers. Matty worked on the tough, wiry captain, but Johnny smashed a low sinking liner to left. Outfielder George Burns charged the ball but he couldn't snare it, and it went for a two-bagger. Josh Devore and Herbie Moran scampered home, ending the game at 5-4 and putting the Braves alone in first place again.

They stayed there only during the lunch hour, however. That afternoon, after the ball park had been cleared of fans and then filled to the rafters again, the Braves took a bad beating. Behind the steady pitching of Jeff Tesreau, McGraw's men allowed only one run while they ran up 10.

Feeling between the teams ran high in this game. They traded insults on the playing field and back and forth from the dugouts. Fred Snodgrass, the Giants' center fielder, almost started a riot. After getting his arm nicked by a pitch thrown by Lefty Tyler, Fred thumbed his nose at Lefty as he trotted to first.

This so angered the Boston fans that they greeted him with a shower of pop bottles when he returned to center field. Things were getting out of hand. James M. Curley, the mayor of Boston, stormed on the field and demanded that Snodgrass be removed on charges of attempting to incite a riot. The chief umpire refused to oust the player. McGraw, however, took Snodgrass out to save him from serious injury.

Again the Braves and the Giants were locked in a tie for

first place. They would not be tied after the third and final game the next day, though. One or the other would be on top by a full game.

When the teams faced each other in the finale, they were deadly serious. The Snodgrass incident was quickly forgotten. The bench jockeys were quieter than usual.

McGraw named Rube Marquard as his starting pitcher. This was a surprise because the Rube had not been doing well for the Giants. Normally a brilliant pitcher, he was on a losing streak. But McGraw had a strong hunch that he was way overdue for a victory and would deliver one for the Giants.

There was no question about who would pitch for the Braves. It was Bill James' turn to start, and he was ready.

Both McGraw and Stallings were on edge when Snodgrass went out to take his place in center field. They feared that the hostile fans might injure him and disrupt the game. But nothing happened. They did not even boo him. Indeed, when Snodgrass made a great running catch off Hank Gowdy, the fans gave him an ovation.

Bill James' spitter was working beautifully that afternoon. The Giants were baffled by it. They only got three hits and the Braves won easily, 8 to 3.

Once more the Braves were on top, and this time they stayed there. It was no longer a race after that. The Braves continued their rampage and finished out of sight, 10½ games in front of the second-place Giants.

This meant a gain of 25½ games in about half the season. It was a most remarkable turnabout. Their record in the first half of the season was 34 won, 43 lost; their second-half record was 60 won, 16 lost.

Some baseball writers could hardly believe it. One of them wrote that the Braves' triumph was a fluke. "A fluke, eh?" Stallings barked at the writer. "It's no fluke when you beat the best clubs in the game from the middle of July to the middle of October."

Hank Gowdy had this to say: "The pitching we got from the Big Three counted most. They had guts and they got the ball over the plate in the pinch. They had perfect control. They could throw through the eye of a needle."

Here is what they did from mid-July on, when the chips were down: They won 49 games and lost only 10. Bill James won 19 of his last 20 games. Dick Rudloph had a 12-game winning streak. Lefty Tyler, the flame-thrower, was just about untouchable.

Modest Bill James offered his opinion. "Man for man we weren't great," he said. "We belonged in eighth place when we were there, and without Stallings we belonged there at the end of the season."

Stallings, of course, could not have done it all by himself. But undoubtedly he set the fire that inflamed the Braves. And the peppery Johnny Evers, the "holler guy" fighting for every point, fanned the flames and kept the fire going on the field.

So the pennant was theirs at last. That in itself seemed a miracle. But now came the supreme test. They were going to tangle with the mighty Philadelphia Athletics, a powerful team that had just won their fourth American League pennant in five years and had three world championships under their belt. They had never lost a World Series.

Under the shrewd management of Connie Mack, the star-studded Athletics boasted an incomparable infield and one of the finest pitching staffs ever assembled. The club was loaded with future Hall of Famers: pitchers Herb Pennock, Eddie Plank and Chief Bender, a Chippewa Indian; also second baseman Eddie Collins and Home Run Baker on third. Stuffy McGinnis on first hardly knew what an error was. He didn't make a single one in his record stretch of 163 consecutive games of perfect fielding.

Sports writers and fans throughout the nation picked the veteran champion Athletics to demolish the Boston upstarts. Late in the regular season when the pennants had been clinched, bettors made the A's a two-to-one favorite.

Then, on the last Saturday of the season the odds went to three to one. The Braves' slugging third baseman, Red Smith, had broken his ankle, and was out of the Series. This was, indeed, a serious blow. Smith had joined the Braves in mid-season and was hitting at a .314 pace. Stallings was forced to put the .210-hitting Charlie Deal on third.

There was now only one .300 hitter on the club. He was Joe Connolly, who was batting .306 and played left field. But Stallings was not discouraged. "We'll take the A's in four straight games," he told his players.

Connie Mack wanted to be sure that wouldn't happen. He was worried about his players being overconfident. Some of his stars were contemptuous of their foes. Mack told star pitcher Chief Bender to go to New York and scout the Braves in their closing games with the Giants.

The Chief disappeared for a few days, but he did not go to New York. He stayed in Philadlephia and had a holiday. Mack found out about it and was furious.

"What's the use of scouting the Braves?" smiled the big Indian. "They are bush leaguers. We'll have no trouble with them."

The Philadelphia A's famous infield of 1914 were (left to right): Stuffy McInnis (1b), Eddie Collins (2b), Jack Barry (ss) and Home Run Baker (3b).

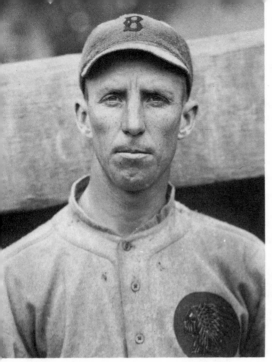

Hank Gowdy, the Braves' red-headed catcher, was the hero of the 1914 World Series. He batted .545, the highest Series mark up to that time.

Chief Bender, a Chippewa Indian, was the A's star pitcher. He faced the Braves in the Series opener in 1914 but did not finish the game.

The Series opened in Philadelphia on October 9 before a crowd of 20,562 in Shibe Park. Mack called upon Chief Bender to pitch. It was the Indian's 10th start in World Series play. He had won six games, lost three and had never been knocked out of the box in a Series game.

But the crafty Chippewa was off in control that day. It did not take long for the Braves to get to him. The miracle men put two runs across in the second inning on successive hits by first baseman Butch Schmidt, Hank Gowdy and the Rabbit.

The A's got one run in their half of the second, although it was unearned due to an error by Johnny Evers. It was their only run of the game, thanks to the coolness and perfect control of the 160-pound hurler, Dick Rudolph. Dick was stingy with his hits. He held the A's to just five scattered blows.

The Braves picked up their second run in the fifth. Until then the Chief was holding up fairly well, but in the sixth the Braves delivered the knockout punch. Evers and Connolly singled, then center fielder Possum Whitted stepped to the plate and smashed a mighty triple to left field, thus driving in two runs. That made the score, 5-1, but there was more to come.

Butch Schmidt singled and brought in Possum Whitted for the Braves' sixth run. That was all for the Chief. Connie Mack, scowling with displeasure, waved the Indian off the mound and summoned a rookie, Weldon Wycoff, to take over. With his head bowed, the humiliated Chief trudged slowly toward the clubhouse. It was the first time in World Series history that an Athletic pitcher had been blasted off the mound.

"Pretty good hitters for bush leaguers, aren't they, Chief?" taunted Conne Mack as the Indian sought the showers. It was the Chief's last game for the A's.

In the eighth inning the Braves got another run, which put them in front, 7 to 1, and that was the final score. The weak-hitting Braves made 11 hits, and just to rub it in they stole three bases, including a double steal by Hank Gowdy and Butch Schmidt—the slowest men in the club. Hank had a perfect day at the plate, with a single, double, triple, and walked twice. A .234 hitter in the season, the tall redhead was to bat .545 in the Series. It was the highest average up to that time. He promptly became known as "Hammering Hank." *

The first game was a frolic for the Braves, but not the second one. It was a squeaker, a classic pitching duel between two fine hurlers. It was veteran Eddie Plank, a southpaw, for the Mackmen versus Big Bill James, king of the spitters.

Eddie Plank had been a dependable and consistant winner for years in regular season games, but he had poor luck in the Series. He had pitched in three Series before this one and had won two games against four defeats. In all four losses his side had not come through with a single run. Of course, a pitcher cannot win no matter how good he is if his team can't get a run for him.

Fans were wondering as Eddie warmed up in Shibe Park for the second game if bad luck would still pursue him. It began to look that way after a few innings. The A's were powerless at

* The nickname was revived some 50 years later by another Brave—Hammering Hank Aaron, the home-run king.

the plate. But then, the Braves weren't doing much either. Both pitchers were sharp and steady. Neither team could score.

So the game went until the top of the eighth inning. The Rabbit grounded out. Then Deal, the weak-hitting substitute for Red Smith, poked out a fluke double. Center fielder Amos Strunk should have caught the ball for an easy out. But he misjudged it and it fell to earth. Plank then fanned James for the second out.

Then came a frightful misplay—bad break number two for the A's. Deal strolled too far off second and catcher Wally Schang had him trapped—or so it seemed. But instead of charging out to the base with the ball, Schang made a long, high throw to Jack Barry at second. Deal saw there was no chance to get back to the bag, so he sprinted for third and made it safely.

Another bad break for the A's quickly followed. Les Mann, the Braves' right fielder, arched a puny fly just in back of Eddie Collins' position at second. Eddie quickly back pedaled, jumped for the ball and got his fingers on it, but he couldn't hold it. As it trickled away for a single, Deal came home and put the Braves ahead, 1 to 0.

There was still a chance for the A's to tie the game, and even win it, in their half of the ninth. And it began to look as if they were going to do just that when James walked Jack Barry. He fanned Schang, but gave another pass to Jim Walsh, a pinch-hitter. Up came Eddie Murphy, the A's leadoff man. He smashed a screamer through the box. It looked like a sure hit. The base runners were on the move—and so was the Rabbit. Far to his left he scurried and made a desperate stab at the ball behind second. He scooped it up, flipped it to Evers who stepped on the bag then rifled the ball to Butch Schmidt at first. It was a double play. The game was over. The Rabbit's acrobatic catch had saved it.

Lady Luck again had frowned upon Eddie Plank. For the fifth time in Series play his teammates had failed to get a run for him. Bill James was at his best that day. He allowed only two hits, a double by Schang in the sixth and a scratch single by Collins in the seventh.

The next set of games would be played in Boston. "Pack the

trunks and send them home to stay," Stallings ordered at the club's hotel in Philadelphia. "We won't be back this way."

After a one-day pause allowed for travel, the teams met in Fenway Park on October 12, a Monday. Some 36,000 fans jammed the park to greet the miracle men and the battered Athletics.

The game turned out to be a grueling, see-saw battle that had the fans standing on their seats half the time. In many respects, it was the best game of the Series.

Lefty Tyler, the third ace of the Big Three, started for the Braves. He was opposed by Bullet Joe Bush, a 21-year-old right-hander with a good fast ball.

The A's broke their long string of 16 scoreless innings by getting a run in the first inning. That put them in the lead for the first time in the Series. They didn't hold it very long, however. The Braves tied the game in the second, and then each team picked up a run in the fourth. That made the score, 2-2, and from then on the teams remained deadlocked through the ninth inning and into the 10th.

As the inning got underway, Lefty Tyler began to lose his touch. He walked Schang and Eddie Collins. Then Eddie Murphy laid down a perfect bunt and made first. When Home Run Baker came up the bases were filled. He drove a deep infield single to Johnny Evers. Schang scored easily from third. Evers had the ball but for some reason he held on to it as if he were in a trance. Realizing this, Eddie Murphy also ran home. The A's now had a 4-to-2 lead.

All seemed lost when the Braves came to bat in their half of the 10th. But Hank Gowdy, who had hit only three homers all season, blasted one into the center-field bleachers. Bullet Joe Bush then fanned pinch-hitter Devore, but walked Herbie Moran.

Evers was up next. Eager to atone for his misplay, Johnny rapped a sharp single through the infield and sent Moran to third. Joe Connolly, a clutch-hitter of note, promptly brought Moran home with a long fly, and again the score was tied.

Lefty Tyler was out of the game. He had been removed for pinch-hitter Devore and Bill James took his place on the mound in the 11th inning. He held the A's scoreless and Bullet Joe did the same to the Braves when his turn came.

The Boston Braves Miracle Team of 1914

(Top Row) Bill James, Ted Cather, Charles Deal, George Davis, Ensign S. Cottrell, Eugene Cocrehan, Otto Hess, Leslie Mann, Hank Gowdy, Charles Schmidt and Bert Whaling.

(Middle Row) George Whitted, Oscar Dugey, George Tyler, Paul Strand, Josh Devore, Larry Gilbert, Red Smith and Herb Moran.

(Bottom Row) Joe Connelly, Fred Mitchell, Batboy Willie Connor, Dick Rudolph, Rabbit Maranville, Dick Crutcher, Bill Martin and Johnny Evers.

The teams were still deadlocked, 4-4, when Hank Gowdy came to bat in the gathering dusk of the 12th inning. He was the first Brave up and he wasted no time. *Whack!* Hank smacked Bullet Joe's pitch into left for a ground-rule double. Stallings sent in Les Mann to run for the slow-footed catcher. Larry Gilbert, batting for Bill James, got a walk. With none out, Herbie Moran tried to bunt the runners along, but he rolled the ball right back to Bullet Joe. The pitcher pounced on it, then threw to third wildly in foul territory. Grinning widely, Les Mann pranced home with the winning run, which gave the Braves a 5-4 victory and made it three straight.

It was a gala day for Hammering Hank and Bill James. Hank hit a homer and a pair of doubles in four times at bat. Bill pitched two hitless innings and was credited with his second Series victory in successive games. In all, he had yielded only two hits and no runs in 11 innings.

The once invincible Athletics were cooked after the third game, and they knew it. They gave up without a fight. Stallings sent in Dick Rudolph, winner of the first game, to make it a cleanup. He went all the way and allowed the A's seven scattered hits, walked one and struck out seven. The lone Athletic run came in the fifth inning on shortstop Jack Barry's single (his

29

first and only hit of the Series in 14 at-bats), and pitcher Bob Shawkey's double.

The Braves had scored one run in the fourth. They shoved two more across in the fifth after two outs on a single by Rudolph, a double by Moran and a timely single by Johnny Evers. It took only an hour and 49 minutes for the Braves to complete the 3-to-1 victory.

For the first time in history the Series was over in four games. Stallings had called upon his Big Three pitchers and no others. Rudolph and James each won two games.

The inspired Braves had never played better ball. The pitching was unsurpassed, their defense was tight and they hit way over their heads. Hammering Hank was the first player to hit over .500 in a Series. Johnny Evers was close to him with .438, and the Rabbit, who batted .246 in the season, hit .307.

Baseball has never seen anything quite like the Miracle Braves of 1914. In 1950 at the mid-century mark, the Associated Press polled the leading sports writers of the nation to choose the greatest upset in any sport of the first 50 years of this century. The performance of the Miracle Braves won by the whopping margin of 128 votes to 53.

They have since become a symbol for the underdog, the living proof that anything is possible if the will to win is there. They were as spirited a group of athletes as ever banded together.

Spirit. That's what the Braves had and the Athletics lacked. It is a difficult word to define. Chief Bender knew the meaning of the word. Here is what he said many years after he faced the Braves in the 1914 Series:

"Spirit is something you cannot buy or cannot learn. It is like a tonic. You don't know where it comes from when you have it and you don't know where it goes when you lose it. The Boston Braves had that kind of spirit that year. It wasn't mere combativeness. It was confidence and determination mixed. And that's a hard nut to crack."

2

The New York Giants

The Blow Heard 'Round the World

IN THE FIRST 50 years of this century baseball had produced only one club worthy of the name, "Miracle Team." It was, indeed, a baseball rarity; most fans could not believe that there would ever be another one.

But history has a way of repeating itself. The second half of the century had barely started when along came a club that set the baseball world on fire.

The team was the New York Giants of 1951. Like the 1914 Braves, it was not a great club, but it was solid. It had good pitching, a fair defense and a couple of .300 hitters. And it had Bobby Thomson.

Whenever oldtimers get together and talk about the 1951 Giants, the name most frequently mentioned is Bobby Thomson. His name has a special place in all the baseball histories along with such titans as Joe DiMaggio, Stan Musial and Ted Williams. His bat is in the Baseball Hall of Fame at Cooperstown, the one he swung one cloudy afternoon in October and struck the "Blow Heard 'Round the World."

Bobby Thomson was born in Glasgow, Scotland, on October 25, 1923, the youngest of six children of Scottish parents. He was baptized Robert Brown Thomson but nobody ever called him that. He was always "Bobby" and that is how he is listed in the official records in the "Encyclopedia of Baseball."

Bobby was a toddler when his mother brought him to this country with his four sisters and his brother, Jim. He never had any recollection of his native Scotland, or of the long voyage across the ocean to America.

Bobby's father, a carpenter, had come to this country a few years before and had settled on Staten Island, a part of New York City. He built a home there, then sent for his wife and children, as he had promised them he would.

Bobby's first recollection in life was catching a ball tossed at him by his father and brother in their back yard. During the years their father lived alone in America, he had become a baseball fan. Almost every Sunday afternoon in summer he took his sons to sandlot and semi-pro games on Staten Island.

Jim recognized his brother's natural talents right away. "He was just one of those kids who looked like a ballplayer when he walked out on the field," said Jim. "He had a loose, easy way of handling himself. You didn't have to be a scout to see that the kid had it."

One afternoon though, George Mack, a scout for the New York Giants, was watching a Sunday league game on the island. He was not there to look over any particular player, but he was impressed by the way Bobby handled himself at shortstop and at the plate.

After the game he met Bobby, who was then 18 and in his senior year at high school. The scout asked him if he'd like to come to the Polo Grounds for a tryout.

Would he? Bobby's head was spinning in excitement. The Giants were his favorite team. Many times he had sat in the bleachers rooting for them. "You bet I'll be there," he told Mack.

A few days later he was in his baseball suit on the very field where his heroes played. Giants coaches Dolph Luque and Pancho Snyder watched Bobby go through a fielding drill at

Bobby Thomson, outfielder-third baseman for the New York Giants in 1951, picks out one of his favorite bats in the dugout at the Polo Grounds. *Wide World Photos*

shortstop. They nodded approval to each other. "Looks like this kid might make it," commented Snyder.

Shortly afterwards on a bright June day, Bobby signed with the Giants to play Class D, minor-league ball at $100 a month. The next day he graduated from Curtis High School in Staten Island.

His first season in Class D ball (rated the lowest in the minors) was a mixture of confusion and disappointment, but it had its high notes.

The Bristol manager worked Bobby at third for five games. He was doing all right, he thought, but then the manager told him that he was being transferred to Rocky Mount, a Class D club in North Carolina. The team needed a third baseman, he was told.

Rocky Mount was playing in Danville, Virginia, when Bobby joined his new club. He played a game there and boarded the club bus for the return trip to Rocky Mount. On the way, a stop was made for a quick meal at a roadside diner. Bobby was munching a hot dog by himself, when he looked up and saw to his horror that the bus had gone. No one remembered he was on the team.

Frantically, he dashed out onto the highway, only to see the bus disappearing on the horizon. It was a dark moment for him.

By luck, a state trooper was in the diner and he saw it all. He offered to catch the bus for Bobby. In no time he was back on it again. As he took his seat, he jokingly said to his new manager, "Gee, have you given up on me so soon?"

He gave the team reason to remember him in his first time at bat in Rocky Mount. He hit a homer. Disappointment soon followed, however. The club already had a good third baseman and Bobby sat on the bench a lot.

He wrote discouraged letters to his brother in Staten Island. Jim answered with pep talks. "Show them something," he wrote. "Don't just fret on the bench and get discouraged."

Bobby played more often in the last part of the season. He got into 29 games and although he hit only .241, he batted in 18 runs in 21 hits. His high ratio of RBIs to number of hits is noteworthy. It is typical of his hitting during his entire career. When runners were on base, his batting average would soar to around .400. When the bases were empty he was usually weak at the plate.

Bobby ended his Rocky Mountain days on a high note. In the last playoff game he came through with the winning home run. The joyous fans passed the hat around in the stands and gave the contents to Bobby: $10.

At this point his baseball career came to a halt. He was drafted. He served the next three years in the Army Air Force, but he was never in combat as he was not sent out of the United States. The only time his life was endangered was the night his barracks suddenly burst into flames and everyone had to rush for the exits. The first and only thing Bobby grabbed on his way out was his infielder's glove.

He left the service as Lieutenant Robert B. Thomson and went home to Staten Island. He was ready to start all over again in Class D ball, but the Giants had other plans for him. They sent him to Jacksonville, Florida, the testing grounds for their Jersey City farm club. This was AAA-rated baseball, the highest in the minors.

In Jacksonville Bobby quickly showed that he could outrun everybody in camp. His speed impressed the Giants' staff. They told him to work in the outfield. But Bobby was unhappy out "in the garden." It was lonely out there and things were slow. He missed the constant action and pep talks of the infield. Besides, he knew he wasn't very good at judging flies. Despite this, the coaches decided that he deserved a chance to play on the Jersey City Giants.

What Bobby feared most happened on opening day in Jersey City before a capacity crowd. A long fly ball came sailing out his way. It should have been an easy out for him, but he misjudged the ball. It flew by him and the batter got an undeserved triple.

Manager Bruno Betzel put Bobby on third where he belonged. He played most of the season there and finished with a .280 batting average. Even though he was below .300, he was the best batter on the team. The weak-hitting, "Little Giants" were in eighth place in the International League.

The league's batting champion that year was Jackie Robinson, also a rookie. He hit .349 for Montreal. Bobby's run production, however, was much better than Jackie's. Bobby was credited with 92 RBIs and 26 home runs; Jackie had 66 RBIs and only three homers.

Toward the end of the season the parent Giants brought Bobby to the Polo Grounds to play a few games. Although the Giants had been a consistently good club over the years, they were at a low ebb when Bobby joined them in 1946. They were in last place and they knew that they would finish there.

For this reason there wasn't much pressure on Bobby in the unimportant games he played as a substitute third baseman. He was loose and confident, yet thrilled beyond description to be a Giant, a *real* Giant in the big time, the National League.

Another thrill was the presence of the great Mel Ott, Bobby's

Mel Ott managed the Giants for 7 years. He was popular everywhere, even with Brooklyn foes.

boyhood hero. "Little Mel," as the 5-foot, 9-inch superstar was called by his admiring fans for more than 20 years, was only 17 when he came to the Giants in 1926. The Giants' uniform was the only one he wore for the next 22 years. He became the playing manager in 1942.

Mel liked the free, full cut that Bobby took at the ball, and his eagerness in covering third. He told the brown-haired infielder to keep in shape that winter so that he could give a good account of himself next spring at the Giants training quarters in Phoenix, Arizona.

All winter long, four or five days a week, Bobby rowed alone across the empty waters of the Great Kills harbor off Staten Island. He was convinced that rowing was one of the best ex- exercises for building up his forearms and developing his back muscles.

The baseball writers in Phoenix wrote pages about Bobby when he joined the Giants at training quarters in March, 1947. He was immensely popular with them.

"A lighthearted kid with the warmest personality you can imagine," wrote a veteran reporter. "He's serious-minded, yet full of humor. Everyone likes him," said another sportswriter. Their opinion of him never changed with the passing of the seasons.

Bobby found himself in a three-cornered race for third base that spring. His rivals were Jack Lohrke, a rookie full of pepper, and the experienced Sid Gordon, who had played in the outfield and at third.

Mel Ott decided that each would be given an equal chance at playing third. They would be rotated at the position in ex- hibition games.

As the test continued, Lohrke seemed to have the best glove, although he was a poor hitter. Sid Gordon could be depended upon to hit close to .300. His bat was needed badly. He could switch to the outfield. What was left for Bobby? Jersey City again?

That's the way it looked to the Giant players when they saw Mel and Bobby seated on the ground after an exhibition game, talking earnestly with each other. The start of the regular season was only a week off.

Bobby knew that the players were watching him and Mel. "I knew what they were thinking," Bobby recalled. "They figured Mel was giving me the bad news and I'd be going back to Jersey City. But he was really asking me if I could play second base. I told him I never had, but I'd like to give it a try."

Bobby was faced with the tough job of having to prove himself at a strange position. There were times that season when he wished he had been sent back to Jersey City. Opening Day was one of those times.

The Giants were in the field and there was a runner on first, Nobody out. In this situation, shortstop Bill Rigney was to give the sign for covering second. If he opened his mouth, that meant Bobby was to cover the bag; if Rigney kept his mouth closed, he himself would cover. Here is how Bobby remembers the play:

"A guy gets on first and I look to Rig, and he has his mouth open. All of a sudden, I can't remember whether open-mouth is me covering or him. As a result, neither of us covered and (catcher) Cooper threw the ball into centerfield. It was a big fat double-play ball that Cooper threw away, and I just stood there looking at it."

However, Bobby made amends for his boner by poling out two homers that day. He played second in only nine games, and he made five errors. Mel put him out in center field for the rest of the season.

His defensive play was ragged, and he sometimes threw to the wrong base. But he had dazzling speed and he was walloping the ball. He finished the season with a .283 batting average, 85 RBIs and 29 homers. Not bad at all for a rookie.

The Rookie of the Year Award went to Jackie Robinson, the Dodgers' first baseman, and incidentally, the first Negro to play major-league ball in this century. Jackie batted .297 and led the league with 29 stolen bases.

Great things were expected of Bobby as the 1948 season approached. He was at the top of his form in the spring training games out west. The pitchers could not get him out. His batting average rose to a sizzling .475 when the Giants left Phoenix. His teammates were sure that he'd lead the club in batting in the regular season.

But they had not figured on an ailment that commonly besets a second-year man who has enjoyed a very good rookie year. It is known in the baseball world as the "sophomore slump." It is a severe letdown.

After the spring hot streak, Bobby suddenly cooled off. He could not hit. His average fell below .250. In the outfield he seemed to be lazy and indifferent. "He looks asleep out there," said Mel Ott, and benched him. Bobby could not understand what had gone wrong and was in anguish.

DUROCHER REPLACES MEL OTT

SPORTING FINAL
★★★★★
STOCK EXCHANGE CLOSING
AND BID AND ASKED PRICES

The  Sun

SEVENTH SPORTS
Tomorrow's Entries and Selections
LATEST RACING RESULTS
U. S. Weather Bureau Forecast:
Mostly sunny today; cloudy tonight; showers tomorrow.
Temperatures Today—Min., 64.5; Max., 81.
Expected in City Tomorrow—Min., 70; Max., 82.
Sun rises 5:38 A. M. Sun sets 8:25 P. M.
(Detailed weather report on page 21.)

VOL. 115—NO. 269.

Entered as Second Class Matter
Post Office, New York, N. Y.

NEW YORK, FRIDAY, JULY 16, 1948.

FIVE CENTS EVERYWHERE

He was further disturbed by the startling news that Mel Ott would be replaced by Leo Durocher on July 16. The whole baseball world was shaken by this announcement. Durocher was the manager of the Brooklyn Dodgers. A bitter rivalry had existed between the Giants and the Dodgers for 50 years.

The Giants had always looked down upon the Dodgers as their poor country cousins. The Dodgers, also known as the Bums, played in a shabby little park far from glittering Manhattan and the spacious Polo Grounds. They were the clowns of the National League. They were losers. They had won only four pennants in 48 years and had yet to win a World Series.

Leo (Lippy) Durocher, manager of the Giants, never lost faith in his team, even when it was 13 ½ games behind the Dodgers in mid-August.
Wide World Photos

The Giants, on the other hand, were traditionally the glamour club of the big city. They had style and they were winners. They had come forth with great stars and they had won more pennants than any other National League team. The Giants took care of their own. After Mel quit managing (at his own request), he stayed in the Giant organization to the end of his days.

Loud-mouthed "Lippy" Durocher, so named because of his constantly wagging tongue, was an abusive umpire baiter, a fist fighter and the 'holler guy" on the four clubs he had played. Trouble seemed to follow him around. He was suspended from baseball for a year by Commissioner Happy Chandler for his general bad conduct on and off the field.

Oldtime Giants fans were horrified at the thought of his coming to the Polo Grounds. To them it was like giving command of the U.S. Army to an enemy general during a war.

But Leo knew baseball, he knew how to handle players and he was a hard worker. In time, the Giant fans stopped booing him and half accepted him.

The new manager had words of encouragement for Bobby, who was still down in the dumps. Leo took him aside and said, "Look, you're young. You've got talent. You can run, throw and hit the long ball. We can do something with those things."

Bobby's only real weakness was poor base running. For all his speed, he was slow to learn the art of rounding the bases at full tilt. He ranked way down the list as a base stealer. Yet he ran like a sprinter in the outfield when he chased down flies.

No one could touch him in a match race. His teammates were forever trying to promote races for him in spring training games so that they could bet on him. He went up against the fastest runners the other clubs could produce. The Giants backed him to the limit and they never lost on him.

At West Point, where the Giants played a practice game against the Army every spring, Bobby was matched against the fastest man on the football team. He was Vic Pollock, a 165-pound halfback streak. Bobby had never run against a football speedster before.

An 85-yard course down the right-field foul line was measured off and the two runners went to the starting mark.

40

Pollock took the crouching position of a sprinter; Bobby stood upright. At the starter's command, "Go!" Pollock burst from the mark and took the lead. Bobby soon caught up with him and the two ran even for 40 yards. Neither could gain an inch. Then Bobby's stride seemed to widen and he began to pull away. Steadily he opened the gap and at the finish he was far in front.

The Baseball Commissioner heard about these running duels and the large amount of money that was bet on them, and he didn't like it. He promptly banned them.

Mel Ott had brought the Giants from eighth place in 1946 to fourth place the next year, then to fifth place with Durocher in 1948. In Leo's first full season as manager in 1949, the club remained in fifth place. But next year (1950) they climbed to third. It was their best showing in nine years.

Meanwhile, Bobby was having his ups and downs. Following his brilliant rookie year and his dismal sophomore performance, he had a whale of a season in 1949. Playing center field he batted .309, his highest average ever; he hit 27 homers and batted in 108 runs. He was the Giants' top man in all three divisions.

But in 1950, as the Giants edged toward the top, he had another poor year. It was the same old theme; his batting fell off. He was down as far as .230 in September, but Mel Ott, his old manager, helped him with a new batting stance and he broke the slump. Even so, he ended the season with a lukewarm .252. It was discouraging.

The Giants finished third, only five games behind the league-leading Phillies and three games in back of the hated Dodgers. Bobby's weak bat had made the difference. If he had swung it as he had the year before, the pennant would have been waving in the Polo Grounds. And the writers wouldn't be saying that he was an in-and-outer—good one year, not so good the next year.

"I was lousy at bat," he admitted, "but I knew I was helping with my glove. I honestly think I played my best outfield that summer (1950). I was in close and caught a lot of balls I never caught before. I tried hard to avoid being an every-other-year ballplayer."

It was true that Bobby had become one of the best defensive outfielders in the game. Now if he could only combine his defensive skills with some good batting, the Giants would have an excellent chance of coming home in front. The Dodgers, however, were the heavy favorites as the 1951 season approached.

Durocher saw the race as a close one between the Giants and the Dodgers. He had put together an aggressive, hustling club that was only fair in hitting but strong in pitching. "It's my kind of a team," he told reporters.

It didn't look like the kind of a team that anybody would want, judging on its performance the first two weeks of the season. The Giants lost the opener, then won the next game, then went into a tailspin and lost 11 games in a row! In no time they were in the basement and the Dodgers were gazing down upon them from the top floor.

They were, of course, better than that. In the next few weeks they began a slow climb up the ladder. But the Dodgers were yielding no ground at all. They were firmly in first place and showed no signs of weakening. They had two of the best pitchers in the league in Schoolboy Roe (22-3) and Don Newcombe (20-9), and an array of topnotch hitters like Jackie Robinson (.338) and catcher Roy Campanella (.325), named Most Valuable Player that year.

Gil Hodges, the fielding genius who hit 40 homers, was at first; veteran Pee Wee Reese was still going strong at short, and Billy Cox, the gifted glove man, was at third. There was no weakness in the Dodgers' all-around capable outfield: graceful Duke Snider, Andy Pafko and Carl Furillo, the rifle-armed right fielder.

It was one of the classiest of all Dodger teams, and they looked it as they threatened to make a runaway of the race.

As for the Giants, they were still in last place as late as May 15. Bobby was not much help to them with his lowly .237 average. The best thing going for them was Durocher's steadfast belief in his players. He took the jibes of the fans and the newspapermen and refused to give up or concede a thing. He kept experimenting with the club, making changes here and there, shifting positions and constantly infusing his players with fighting spirit.

When Monte Irvin, a .312 slugger, failed to deliver at first base, he moved Whitey Lockman there and shifted Irvin to the outfield. This change helped both players and strengthened the club.

In another inspired move, he brought Bobby from the outfield to third base in place of the slumping Hank Thompson. It was Bobby's favorite position, but he hadn't played it for four years. No matter, he soon became one of the best third sackers in the game and his hitting, like Irvin's, picked up remarkably.

Late in May, when the Giants began edging upwards, Leo picked up the phone one night and called Tommy Heath, manager of the Minneapolis Millers of the high-ranking American Association. On the club playing center field was a promising youngster who had just turned 20 and was beginning his second year in the minors. He was a Giant property named Willie Howard Mays, Jr. Leo told Heath that he thought he had a place for Willie and to send him on to New York right away.

Later, when Willie was told that Heath wanted to see him, he reported to his manager's hotel room. Heath was standing in the middle of the room, holding out his hand and grinning. "Congratulations!" he said to Willie.

"What for?" asked the ballplayer.

"You're going up to the big league, the Giants."

"Who said so?"

"Leo Durocher."

"Not me," Willie exclaimed. "Call him up and tell him I'm not coming."

Heath thought that Willie had suddenly lost his mind. But as he talked to him he realized that Willie meant what he said. He got Leo on the phone and told him that Willie did not want to leave the Millers. "I can't do anything with him," said Heath. "You talk to him, Leo. I'll put Willie on."

Leo was boiling over in anger. "What do you mean, you're not coming up?" he yelled.

"I mean it," Willie replied. "I can't play that kind of ball yet."

"What do you mean by that exactly?" Leo asked. "What *can't* you do?"

"Hitting," said Willie.

"What are you hitting for Minneapolis now?"

Manager Durocher immediately knew that he had a superstar in the making when Willie Mays (above) joined the Giants as a rookie in May, 1951.

".477."

"Well," said Leo after a pause. His tone was softer. "Do you think you can hit .250 for me?"

".250?" Willie said. "I can try."

"Then come on up here!" shouted Leo.

And that is how Willie came to play for the Giants, and to become in time the greatest Giant of them all in the long history of the club.

He did not look very impressive, however, when he joined the Giants in Philadelphia on May 25 and went hitless in his first three games. Then it was back to New York to face the Boston Braves and their ace hurler, Warren Spahn. Willie, who had gone o for 12 in Philadelphia, got hold of one of Spahn's fast balls and hit it on a line over the left field roof. So, his first major-league hit was a home run.

That's the end of the slump, thought Willie as he joyfully circled the bases before a standing crowd. But it was not to be. Unfortunately for Willie, that home run stood as his only hit in his next 13 at-bats.

He was hitting .038 and was worried sick. Confused and shaken, he went to Leo and asked to be sent back to the minor leagues.

"Why do you want to go back?" asked Leo.

"Because I'm not hitting, that's why. Just like I told you on the phone from Minneapolis."

"Is the pitching any different here?"

"No, there's not that much difference," said Willie. "But if it isn't the pitching, then it must be I'm in a slump. Anyway, I'm not helping you any."

"Listen," Leo said and put his hand on Willie's shoulder. "You can slump in Minneapolis as easy as you can slump up here. We've been winning ball games since you came up, haven't we?"

"Most of them," Willie admitted.

"Then you're my center fielder, and that's that," said Leo with finality.

Right after his talk with Leo, Willie shot out of his slump like a rocket taking off. He got nine hits in his next 24 times up. Now he was hitting at a .375 clip and his worries were over.

The Giants spent 44 days in the second division and did not get up to fourth place until June 3. They stayed in the first division from then on. The team was beginning to jell and was playing better than 500 ball. But the first-place Dodgers were still out of sight and climbing higher. Some experts predicted that Brooklyn would win the pennant by at least 20 games.

The Giants kept plugging away, climbing up the first division ladder and by the middle of June they were in second place. There they stopped as if to get their breath. They were six games behind the Dodgers and they could not narrow the gap. Indeed, the gap grew wider. On the Fourth of July the Dodgers swept a double header from the Giants. That put the Brooks eight and a half games in front.

"We knocked them out," chuckled Charley Dressen, the talkative manager of the Dodgers. "They'll never bother us again."

The Giants were a solid club with some brilliant performers, but try as they might, they could not gain an inch on the Dodgers as July wore into August. On August first they were nine and a half games behind their bitter foes from across the Brooklyn Bridge. Their won-lost record stood at 56-44.

The Giants had a red-hot pitching staff headed by Sal Maglie and Larry Jansen. Sal was known as the Barber because of his razor-sharp control. Steady Larry Jansen was one of the best moundsmen in the league. Both men were 23-game winners that year. Their receiver was hard-working Wes Westrum, who could hit the long ball and was good in the clutch.

Top-ranking Alvin Dark was at short, hitting a healthy .303. At second was little Eddie Stanky, known as the "Brat." He reminded oldtimers of Johnny Evers. A fiery competitor, the Brat swung a puny bat (.244) but he drew more walks than any other player. Leo called him "the best leadoff man in baseball." Bobby Thomson played inspired ball once he was back at his old stand at third. Some writers called him the "Hawk" because of the way he pounced on the scorching drives that sped his way.

The outfield had power and reasonable defensive strength. "Wondrous Willie" Mays captivated New York fans with his sensational running catches in the far reaches of the deepest center field in the majors. Monte Irwin in left field was the club's top slugger. He batted a healthy .312 that year and led the league with 121 RBIs.

With all that talent the Giants should have held their own in their head-on collisions with the Dodgers. But such was not the case. In their 12 meetings, as of August 6, the Dodgers had clobbered the Giants nine times, while losing only three games. At that rate the Giants would most certainly never overcome the Brooks' wide lead.

Now it was August 7 and the Giants were again in Brooklyn, this time for a three-game, do-or-die series. The season was more

Here, Wondrous Willie Mays chases down a long drive that would have been a triple if he had not snared it against the wall in deep center.

than half over. Time was running out. The Giants knew that they must win at least two of the three games if they hoped to stay alive in the race.

They were keyed up for this series. They were thinking in terms of three straight wins. They believed that the impossible was about to happen. And so it did! But, alas, not the way they thought it would.

The Giants dropped the first game; then they took another walloping the next day. And as if that wasn't punishment enough, on the night of August 9 they lost the final game.

The Brooks had beaten the Giants for the twelfth time in 15 meetings. By winning three straight the Dodgers increased their lead to 12½ games.

Leo's discouraged players filed into the dressing room in silence after the final game. They were crushed and were not saying anything. But there was plenty of noise coming through the closed door that separated them from the Brooks' dressing room.

The Dodgers were jubilant. They were whopping it up, singing and shouting. "Eat your heart out, Leo! So that's your kind of a team?" they kept shouting and rubbing it in. They sang loudly in unison, "Roll out the barrels . . . we've got the Giants on the run."

The Giants listened and recognized at least four of the voices. They were Jackie Robinson, Pee Wee Reese, Don Newcombe and outfielder Carl Furillo. The Giants knew them well, because those four had been riding them unmercifully all season.

Through it all, Leo was talking to some newspapermen. They wanted to know if he planned any changes in the lineup. His answer came through the din, and it was clear and loud: "This is my team. There will be no changes in the lineup. If they go down, I go down with them. If they go up, so do I. This is my team and I'm going to stick with it."

Leo had one of the loudest voices in baseball and the Giants heard every word he said. It gave them a big lift. Al Dark, the Giants' team captain, spoke for all the players when he said, "When a manager sticks with his players like that, you have to go all the way for him. I know this team wanted to win the pennant for Leo."

The worst was not over, though. On August 11, two days after the Brooklyn disaster, the Phillies blanked the Giants, 4-0, while the Dodgers were beating Boston, 8 to 1, in the first game of a double header.

At that moment, between the games of the double header, this was the standing:

	W	L	G.B. (Games Behind)
Brooklyn	70	35	—
New York	59	51	13½

That was the absolute low for the Giants. The Dodgers lost the second game of that day's double header, so on the morning of August 12 the Giants were 13 games behind. (On that same day 37 years ago, the Boston Braves were also in second place, but they were trailing by only six and a half games.)

That afternoon (August 12) Leo's men beat the Phillies, 3 to 2. It was Sal Maglie's 16th victory of the season. Then an unknown rookie named Al Corwin took the mound for the

Giants. He had come up from Ottawa in mid-season and had never pitched major-league ball. He was to prove invaluable to the club by reeling off four straight triumphs when they were most needed. The young rookie pitched a four-hitter that afternoon and the Giants won, 2 to 1. It was a good double header to win. "They had better do some winning," wrote a reporter, "if they want to finish second."

The next day Larry Jansen won his 15th game, beating the Phils, 5 to 2. "Wondrous Willie" saved the day by making a diving shoestring nab of a sinking liner hit by Willie Jones.

That made it three straight for the Giants. Were they stirring, beginning to wake up, or was it just a flash? They would soon know. Looming ahead were the Dodgers who would invade the Polo Grounds on August 16 to begin a vital three-game series. So far this season, all the Dodgers had to do to beat the Giants was to show up at the ball park.

Leo's pitcher for the first game was stocky George Spencer,

Pitcher George Spencer was a surprise starter for the critical Giant-Dodger game of August 16. N.Y. *Daily News*

an old Ohio State blocking back. He was a surprise starter, for he was a relief pitcher. He was known as the iron horse of the bull pen because he had appeared in more than 50 games. But today he was out there on the mound getting ready to start the game with his first pitch.

Leo's hunch that George's sidearm stuff might baffle the Brooks was a good one. The durable pitcher went all the way and whipped the Dodgers, 4 to 2. His victory may have been the most important game of the year from the Giants' viewpoint. It broke the Dodger jinx.

With their confidence restored, the Giants beat the Brooks the next day, 3 to 1. Jim Hearn (17-9) was the winner, thanks in great part to Wes Westrum's two-run homer in the eighth. The final game belonged to the Barber, Sal Maglie. He was never sharper as he turned in a 2-to-1 win over Don Newcombe to make a clean sweep of the series.

The Phils were the next visitors to the Polo Grounds. Again Leo picked iron horse George Spencer to start, and again the pitcher came through, this time with an 8-to-5 win. Then on the following day Larry Jansen humbled the Phils, 2 to 0, with a four-hitter, beating the great Robin Roberts in the bargain.

That was on August 19. In the clubhouse after the game Bobby Thomson was the first to ask what everybody wanted to know, "What did the Dodgers do today up in Boston?"

"They lost, 13 to 4. That's a good licking. It'll hurt 'em," someone said.

Al Dark commented, "That means we're now eight games out of first."

"How many have we won in a row now?" somebody asked.

Willie Mays knew the answer to that. "Eight," he said. "Maybe we can keep on going."

That didn't seem possible the next day in the final with the Phils, when the Giants found themselves trailing, 4 to 0, in the seventh inning. But when a club is hot almost anything can happen. The Giants suddenly exploded and put five runs across, winning 5 to 4.

Leo's men were rolling now. Everything they did was right. When hits were needed, they murdered the ball. They staged come-from-behind rallies that left the fans breathless. Their fielders came through with sensational game-saving plays. And their hurlers were bearing down all the way—and winning.

Monte Irvin was the big gun of the Giant drive, coming up with the vital hit in the clutch time and again. Al Dark and Eddie Stanky, the great second base combination, were never better. Al was hitting ferociously and fielding sensationally every game, Eddie didn't get many hits, but he was drawing one, two and three walks a day. Bobby Thomson was belting the ball at a .357 clip after going to third.

Everybody did his bit. And nobody more than Leo, the manager who would never quit.

After the sweep of the Phillies, the western teams came in to the Polo Grounds. Cincinnati was the first club to arrive. The Reds crashed to earth like a flaming plane as the Giants took three games from them. That made it 11 straight wins.

The Cards were next. They came in for a one-game stand. They were leading, 5 to 4, going into the last of the ninth, when *Bam!* the Giants teed off on the hapless Cardinal hurlers and in no time they scored two runs for a 6-to-5 victory. Number 12 for Leo's boys!

The baseball world was sitting up and taking notice now. Fans all over the country were watching the winning streak. But the Dodgers were not concerned. After all, they had been in first place ever since May 13 and they were still there in September, with a sound seven-game lead. The Giants didn't have time enough to catch them, they thought.

Coming up now were four games with the Cubs in the Polo Grounds. They would be played in the form of two double headers on two consecutive days.

The Giants won the first double header, 5 to 4, and 5 to 1. That made it 14 in a row. The next day the steamed-up club was aiming for number 15 in the first game of the scheduled double header. Larry Jansen was on the mound, going all the way for the Giants, but they could not get enough runs for him to break the 3-to-3 tie at the end of the ninth.

By this time the strain on both clubs was tremendous. Something had to give—and it did, in the top of the 12th when the

Cubs put a run across and went ahead, 4 to 3. Victory was in sight for the Cubs as the Giants came to bat in the bottom of the 12th. But the stress was too much for them. Their defense lapsed—not badly, but just enough to enable the Giants to push over two runs and win the game, 5 to 4. In the second game Al Corwin, the remarkable rookie, had his stuff all the way and won it for the Giants, 6 to 3.

They had now won 16 in a row. It was the longest winning streak in the National League in 16 years, since 1935 when Willie Mays was four years old. In the course of the streak, the Giants had cut eight games off the Dodgers' lead.

Next day the streak ended as Leo's men went down to a 2-0 defeat at the hands of the Pirates. That single loss did not bother the Giants at all. They shrugged it off and went right on winning.

Leo kept encouraging his players. He never held clubhouse meetings but he would talk to them in groups at practice sessions or in the dressing room. His target was the hated Dodgers. "Keep after them," he'd say. "Keep the pressure on them and maybe sooner or later they'll crack. You never can tell. Forget everything but the job of winning each game as it comes along. Just go after the game you have to win today. Sooner or later, something will happen."

Something did happen on September 9 when the Giants were playing the Dodgers. Sal Maglie had a comfortable 2-0 lead going into the top half of the eighth. He got Pee Wee Reese out on a pop fly, but then he lost his touch. Duke Snider lashed out a double and Jackie Robinson quickly followed with a triple to deep left. Snider scored, and up came Andy Pafko. Robinson was standing on third. If he got home the game would be tied.

Pafko hit a bullet down the third base line. It seemed unstoppable, good for two bases. But Bobby Thomson saved the day. He smothered it with a backhand stab, lunged across the bag to tag Robinson as he tried to scramble back to third, then reeled to his feet and fired a strike across the diamond to double up Pafko at first.

That killed a big Dodger rally and ended the inning. Leo and coach Freddy Fitzimmons both called it the greatest play they'd ever seen a third baseman make under such pressure.

Pitcher Sal Maglie, nick-
named the Barber be-
cause of his razor-sharp
control. *N.Y. Daily News*

It was plays like this that kept the Giants going—and began
to worry the Brooks. At long last, the Dodgers started to realize
that the Giants had a chance to take it all. It was a slim chance,
to be sure, because there wasn't much time left, but it was
possible. The Dodgers knew this and they grew tight and tense
in the home stretch.

Coming home from the West with only 10 games to play,
the Brooks had a four and a half game lead. They were still
heavily favored to win the flag. Only a complete collapse could
knock them off their perch.

But in their last brief stand in Brooklyn they lost two out
of three to the Phils. Meanwhile, in the Polo Grounds the Giants
were having a field day with the Braves. Larry Jansen beat them,
4 to 1, in the first game for his 21st victory of the year. Then
the Giants battered the Braves twice more to make a clean
sweep of the series.

Now the Brooks' lead was cut to two and a half games.

The the rival clubs hit the road for the last time. The Giants went to Philadelphia to play two games; the Dodgers went to Boston for a three-game series.

On September 25 the Giants won their first game, 5 to 1, behind Jim Hearn and Sal Maglie in a relief role.

On that same night, the Brooks, playing their worst ball of the season, blew a double header to the Braves, 6 to 3 and 14 to 2. The Dodgers' lead had dwindled to one game! Both teams won the next day, and Brooklyn held its slim lead.

Now the Giants had two off days, while the Brooks were due to play in Boston and Philadelphia on successive days. Interest in the stretch run was intense throughout the country. Newspapers, including the quiet *New York Times,* ran the ball scores on page one. At a championship prize fight in New York on a night the Giants were in Philadelphia, the score of the ball game was announced between rounds. It got a bigger yell than the fight did.

Hardly anybody talked about the Yankees who were about to clinch their pennant. Everybody was talking about the Giants. Could they really do it? The Dodgers had four games to play; the Giants had only two scheduled. They would have the agony of sitting still for two days (September 27 and 28) and hoping for a Dodger downfall.

And that is what happened. The Brooks lost to Boston, 4 to 3, with an assist from Umpire Frank Dascoli on a hairline decision at the plate. A furious Dodger team left for Philadelphia with its lead cut to half a game.

The next night the Brooks went into the eighth inning with a 3-to-1 lead. But the Phils' catcher, Andy Seminick, a .227 hitter, evened the score by walloping a two-run homer. Then the Phils got another run in the ninth, and that did it.

The Giants and the Dodgers were now all tied up, each with 94 victories and 58 defeats.

The next day was Saturday, September 29, the next to the last day of the season. Sal Maglie was at his best that afternoon as he shut out the Braves, 3 to 0. Now the Giants had undisputed possession of first place for the first time all season. Their half-game lead did not last long, however. That night Don Newcombe blanked the Phils, 5 to 0, and this put the Dodgers back on even terms with the Giants.

It was Sunday, September 30, the final day of the season. In Boston the Giants edged the Braves, 3 to 2, for Jansen's 22nd win. This meant that the Giants could do no worse than finish in a tie with the Brooks. A Dodger victory would put the two clubs even; a Dodger loss would give the Giants a half-game lead, and the pennant.

On the train going back to New York from Boston, the Giants were getting bulletins on the game that was in progress down in Philadelphia. The Brooks were losing by five runs, they heard, and it was the eighth inning. Then Brooklyn somehow tied the score and the game went into extra innings. The Phils loaded the bases with none out, but they couldn't get a run across. Then, in the top of the 14th, Jackie Robinson hit a homer, and Brooklyn won the game. That meant that the Giants and Dodgers would have a playoff. It also meant that the three New York big-league teams all finished in first place. This had never happened before, or since.

Neither had a pennant drive such as the Giants staged ever happened before. It was an amazing, incredible performance. Under intense, demanding pressure in the final stretch, they won 39 games and lost only eight. They finished the season with seven straight wins.

On October 1, the day after the season's end, the Giants and the Dodgers were at it again, this time in a two of three game playoff.

The playoff had to start right away because the World Series was scheduled to begin on October 4 at Yankee Stadium. That gave the clubs three days to settle things. It was barely enough time, as it turned out.

The toss of a coin determined the site of the first game. Brooklyn won the toss, and manager Charley Dressen chose Ebbets Field, his home grounds. The Dodgers had beaten the Giants nine out of 11 games in Ebbets Field that season.

The Giants were at their best before 30,000 rabid Brooklyn fans in Ebbets Field.

**The New York Giants
in 1951**

(Back Row) Sheldon Jones, George Spencer, Monte Irvin, Jack Kramer, Jim Hearn, Spider Jorgensen, Clint Hartung, Allen Gettel, Bob Thomson, Monte Kennedy, Larry Jansen, Sal Maglie, Bill Rigney, Whitey Lockman.

(Center Row) Wes Westrum, Roger Bowman, Artie Wilson, Dave Koslo, Leo Durocher (Manager), Rafael Noble, Henry Thompson, Don Mueller, Jack Lohrke, Fred Fitzsimmons (Coach).

(Front Row) Frank Shellenback (Coach), Herman Franks (Coach), William Leonard (Batboy), Jack Maguire, Sal Yvars, Alvin Dark, Eddie Stanky.

Jim Hearn pitched a five-hitter to overcome Ralph Branca, Brooklyn's fastball pitcher, and the Giant defense was superb. The Dodgers hit into four double plays. Andy Pafko drew first blood by hitting a homer in the second. That gave the Brooks a 1-0 lead until the fourth, when Bobby Thomson homered after Branca had hit Monte Irvin with a pitch. The score stood at 2-1 until the eighth, when Irvin added another homer for insurance The Giants won, 3 to 1, and looked invincible as they happily departed Brooklyn for the last time.

The next day, they looked like clowns. Giant fans who had followed them all season could not believe that this was the same team. They could not hit, they wilted in the clutch, their fielding was the worst ever (five errors), their pitchers gave up 13 hits (four of which were homers) and allowed 10 runs to cross the plate. The Giants got zero runs. Bobby Thomson had a horrible day. He made a costly error and struck out with bases loaded, when a rally might have turned things around. He did get a two-bagger. It was the Giants' longest drive of the game.

So it all came down to the rubber game on October 3. Everything for which the teams had been fighting for in 156 games for six long months would be settled that afternoon in two or three hours. The winning team that day would be in the Yankee Stadium the next, playing in the World Series.

Even years later Bobby could recall every detail of that day. Just before 10 A.M., he said goodbye to his mother at their Staten Island home and drove his car to the ferry. He was in good spirits. The tough day he had yesterday was out of his system. He was thinking of today's game and how great it would be if he could get three hits. It was not too much to hope for, those three hits. He had been hitting well.

It was a cloudy, raw day. When Bobby got to the Polo Grounds he noticed that the crowd waiting for the gates to open was smaller than the one that was there yesterday. It was probably the threat of rain that was keeping the crowd down, he thought.

Bobby joined his teammates in the clubhouse shortly before

noon. The supposed purpose of the meeting was to discuss the Brooklyn hitters. But since the two clubs had played each other 24 times that season, there was nothing new that anyone could say. Leo told Sal Maglie not to give Gil Hodges anything inside. Later, addressing the team, he said: "We haven't quit all year. We're not going to quit now. Let's go get 'em!"

In the Brooks' dressing room, Charley Dressen told Don Newcombe to keep the ball "low and away from Thomson. Don't let him pull it."

Sal the Barber had beaten the Dodgers five times that season, but he was not very sharp in the first inning. He walked Reese and Duke Snider; then Jackie Robinson lined Sal's first pitch into left, and Reese scored. The Dodgers went ahead, 1-0.

The Barber settled down after that. Newcombe was fast, but not so fast that he couldn't be hit. Whitey Lockman bounced a single through the infield at the start of the second, and Bobby Thomson quickly followed with a sharp hit to left. A rally was in the making, it seemed. But it was immediately stifled. Whitey ran to second on Bobby's single and stayed there, seeing that he could not make third. Bobby with head down and running all-out, rounded first and made for second without looking to see where Whitey was. As he approached the bag, Bobby saw to his horror that Whitey was standing on it. Desperately, he tried to get back to first, but he was tagged out in the rundown.

It was a bush-league boner that Bobby had pulled, and he knew it. Red-faced, he returned to the dugout. His hit had gone for nothing.

When the lights were turned on in the darkening ball park in the third inning, a fan cracked, "Well, now maybe Thomson can see where he's going."

It was a grim, quiet crowd of 34,320 (about 1,500 below capacity) that watched the slow-paced game continue. Bobby doubled in the fifth but stayed on second as Newcombe easily pitched out the inning. Again, his hit was wasted.

Nothing much happened until the bottom of the seventh when Monte Irvin banged out a double with no one on. Whitey Lockman then laid down a bunt in front of the plate. Catcher Rube Walker grabbed the ball and whipped it to Billy Cox at

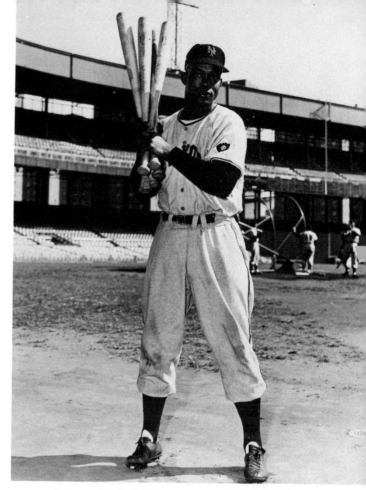

Monte Irvin, the big gun of the Giant drive, came up with vital hits again and again. *N.Y. Daily News*

third, but Irvin beat the throw. Now with runners on first and third, Bobby came to bat for the third time.

Don Newcombe bore down hard and threw only strikes to him. After taking two, Bobby fouled off a fast ball. Then he hit the next one, a high fly into deep center. Irvin scored easily after the catch. There was no play at the plate. Bobby had driven in the Giants' only run. The score was now tied at 1-1, but it didn't stay that way very long.

"My arm's tight," Newcombe complained when he got to the dugout. "I got nothin' left. Nothin'." Roy Campanella, who was out of the game with a sore leg, tried to soothe the big pitcher. "Don't quit on us now, Don. You go out there and burn 'em in for us, Don."

While they were encouraging him, the Dodgers were making life miserable for the Giants. Pee Wee Reese and Duke Snider opened the inning with singles, then Maglie lost control and threw a curve into the dirt. The ball got by catcher Wes Westrum. Reese scored and Snider dashed to third. Sal walked Jackie Robinson and the Dodgers again had men on first and third, with the score, 2 to 1.

Pafko slashed a grounder up the third base line. Bobby moved fast to his right for a backhand try, but the ball bounced off the heel of his glove and went into left field. Snider scored on the single making it 3 to 1 for the Brooks.

Then Bill Cox, batting next, sent a hard, one-hopper toward third. One thought flashed through Bobby's mind: "Get in front of it! Stop it, no matter how!" He would have taken it in the chest or throat, if he had to. But the ball bounced high and streaked over his shoulder into left for another single. In came Jackie to score the Brook's third run of the inning and give them a 4-1 lead.

Newcombe's arm was loose as he burned the ball across the plate in the eighth, and set the Giants down without getting into trouble. Larry Jansen, who replaced the Barber, retired the Dodgers in order in the top of the ninth.

Now it was the last of the ninth as the Giants came to bat. Never had things looked darker for them in that gloomy ball park. Standing on the dugout steps, Leo turned to his players and said quietly, "Well, you've come this far. It's an awful long way to come. And you've still got a chance to hit." Then he trotted out to the third base coaching box and yelled, "Come on! We can still get 'em. Come on!"

This is what the scoreboard showed when Alvin Dark, the first man up, stood at the plate:

Brooklyn   1 0 0 0 0 0 0 3 0
New York   0 0 0 0 0 0 1 0

Newcombe zipped over two quick strikes on Alvin. "I got to get my bat on the ball," he thought. "Must get my bat on it." And he did. On the next pitch he slapped a hard grounder to the right side between Jackie and Gil Hodges. Both men went for it, Jackie playing deep. Newcombe ran over to cover first. Hodges reaching out, touched the ball with the tip of his mitt

60

and deflected it away from Jackie. Had he not touched it, Jackie probably could have made the play. As it was, Alvin was on first with a single.

Next up was outfielder Don Mueller. He hit an almost identical shot through the right side between first and second. Alvin scampered to third. It was the Giants' sixth hit off Newcombe, and they now had runners on first and third.

Charley Dressen walked to the mound. Out in the Dodger bull pen, Ralph Branca and Carl Erskine were throwing. Branca was whizzing over his fast ones, and Erskine's curve was hopping. Dressen chatted with Newcombe for a moment and decided to let him stay in. He went back to the dugout.

Everywhere in the park the fans were on their feet. Monte Irvin, the big clutch-hitter who seldom failed them, was coming up next. He had tagged Newcombe with a double the last time he faced him in the seventh. This time, though, it was a crusher for the fans.

The groans that resounded through the Polo Grounds could be heard several blocks away as Monte put up a meek foul near first. Gil Hodges caught it with ease. Bitterly disappointed, Monte slammed his bat on the ground and kicked up dust. Charley Dressen smiled, feeling that he had made the right decision. Newcombe was doing all right.

Next up was Whitey Lockman. Newcombe gave him an outside fast ball. Whitey went for it and sliced it past third for a double. Alvin Dark tore around from second and got home. Don Mueller sprinting from first to make third, came into the bag with a hard slide. He was safe, but he twisted his ankle. He could not get to his feet. He was taken off the field on a stretcher. Clint Hartung went in to run for him.

The score was now 4 to 2, the Brooks still leading, but the Giants had runners on second and third, with one out and Bobby was getting ready to bat.

Dressen decided that Newcombe was tiring and should be relieved. He came out to the mound. "Who are you bringing in?" asked base umpire Jocko Conlon.

"Branca," said Dressen.

"Branca?" exclaimed the umpire in disbelief. "Why, he's a

fastball pitcher!" The moment he spoke, Conlon regretted his words. He knew he wasn't supposed to question a managerial move, or make any comment on it whatever. It was none of his business. Still, he couldn't help wondering why Dressen wanted Branca instead of Erskine with his hard-to-hit curves. Bobby Thomson would rather face Branca than Erskine any day.

When Branca got to the mound, Newcombe shook his hand earnestly. The big pitcher was cheered as he took the long walk to the center-field clubhouse. Dressen handed Branca the ball and said, "Get him out." Then he turned and walked back to the dugout without saying another word.

Meanwhile, Bobby was waiting patiently for his turn at the plate. He felt sorry about Mueller's injury, but he realized that the delay was helping him to calm down. He strolled over to third, where Leo was standing. "If you ever hit one, hit one now," said Leo.

Going back to the plate, Bobby said to himself, "You're a

Whack! Bobby Thomson connects and the ball sails into the seats above the head of stunned Andy Pafko, the Brook's left fielder (opposite page). *Wide World Photos*

pro, Tom. Act like one. Do a good job." He was concerned only in getting a hit—a single, anything to keep the game alive. And he realized that this was his chance to make up for that wretched base-running he had done in the second inning.

Branca's first pitch was a fast ball, and it cut the center of the plate. Bobby didn't offer at it. "Strike one," umpire Lou Jorda sang out.

The next pitch came in high and inside, not quite as close as Branca wanted it to go. Bobby went for it. He swung hard and socked the ball squarely. It streaked out toward left field. "Get back, get back!" screamed Billy Cox to the outfield as the ball sailed over his head. Left fielder Andy Pafko ran back toward the high wall. "I got a chance at it," he thought.

Willie Mays kneeling in the on-deck circle, watched the ball take off and thought, "This'll get the run in from third." Pafko stopped at the wall; then he turned about and faced the infield. He just stood there, his back to the wall, helpless, as the ball soared into the stands far above his head.

For many seconds the fans sat in silence, as if they were stricken dumb. Willie Mays was motionless, frozen on the spot. They were in momentary shock. They did not realize that this was the game-winning homer. It was the pennant. The game was over. The Giants had won, 5 to 4.

Bobby Thomson jumped up and down like a kangaroo as he circled the bases and made his way home from third, as shown in this photo.

Then came the roar of the crowd—a roar that filled the Polo Grounds and was heard in millions of homes, offices, bars, stores and in the streets all across the nation, wherever people gathered before radio and television sets.

Bobby was now leaping and dancing around the bases. The whole Giant team rushed to the plate to meet him—all except Willie, who still hadn't moved. "It's the pennant! It's the pennant!" he kept yelling.

Andy Pafko in left field stood stunned. As he ambled toward the clubhouse, he kept repeating to himself, "It can't be. It can't be."

Jackie Robinson was the last Dodger to leave the field. He stayed and watched Bobby circle the bases. He wanted to make sure that Bobby touched all the bases before conceding victory to the Giants.

Here, Bobby's teammates pour out of the dugout to greet him just as he steps on the plate to make his historic home run official.

The fans kept cascading out of the stands. The Giants had to push their way through the mob and run for the clubhouse. Even after they got there, the fans stood at least a thousand deep outside the clubhouse windows and chanted for a personal appearance of every Giant. But mainly and repeatedly they yelled for Bobby Thomson, and he obliged time and again by coming out to the top of the clubhouse steps to wave and smile at them.

The Dodger dressing room was like a morgue. There was nothing that anyone could say. Branca sat with his head bowed, silently weeping. He answered a few questions put to him by reporters, then asked them to please leave him alone.

"He felt awful," Charlie Dressen recalled later, "If he'd had a gun I think he would have shot himself." Then pausing for effect, he added, "And if I'd had one, I think I would have given it to him."

Locked in a joyous embrace minutes after Bobby's pennant-winning homer are: Giant's owner Horance Stoneham, Bobby Thomson and Leo Durocher.

Bobby went from the Polo Grounds to a downtown television studio where he appeared before the cameras and was roundly applauded. Everywhere he went he was recognized and cheered. On the ferry to Staten Island passengers spotted him. They surrounded him, shook his hand, patted him.

Through it all, three thoughts raced through his mind: the Giants had won, he had gone over the 100-mark in RBIs for the season, and he had got his three for four that afternoon.

A big crowd was waiting for him at the ferry slip on Staten Island. It took Bobby a long time to get through it gracefully and reach his home in New Dorp. His older brother, Jim, was there waiting for him. When they were alone Jim said quietly, "Bobby, do you realize what you've done?"

Ony then, some six hours after the game, did Bobby become aware of what his big clout meant—that it would be remembered by countless thousands of people for all the rest of his life.

It would be recorded as the most dramatic, all-conclusive home run ever struck by any ball player anywhere. It was as decisive and final as the swing of an executioner's ax to the chopping block; it was the perfect climax to the Giants' miracle, down-the-stretch drive that has no equal in major-league baseball.

The Blow Heard 'Round the World took place on October 3, 1951, at exactly 3:58 P.M. Barely 20 hours later the bone-weary Giants were in Yankee Stadium battling a well-rested and powerful club that had just won its third straight pennant.

This World Series, to almost nobody's surprise, was an anti-climax to the Giants' stunning pennant drive. The fans simply could not get worked up again.

The Giants were not quitting, however. They won two of the first three games, but ran out of miracles after that and lost three straight. That was all.

Bobby Thomson did not shine in the Series. He made two errors, though neither was costly, and got five hits in 21 at-bats for a .238 average. He did not feel too badly about his perform-ance, however.

After all, he had done something for the Giants that would never be forgotten. He had won a pennant for them all by himself, with a single swipe of his bat.

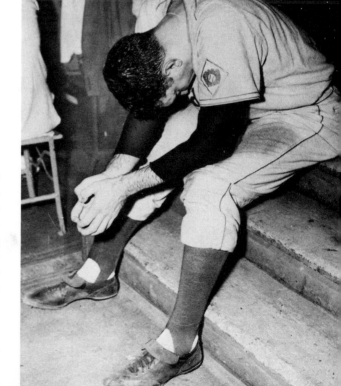

In the Dodger dressing room all was gloomy. Above, Ralph Branca who served Bobby the home-run ball, weeps silently in front of his locker. New York Post photograph by Stein. © 1951, New York Post Corporation

The New York Mets

From Clowns to Champions

ONE MORNING not long after Bobby's famous clout, the baseball world was startled by the headlines on the sports pages. They ran like this:

> BRAVES TO QUIT BOSTON FOR MILWAUKEE
> WILL PLAY THERE IN 1953
> FIRST FRANCHISE MOVE IN 50 YEARS

For more than half a century not one of the 16 major league clubs had moved from its original home. Ever since the American League was formed in 1901, they had remained where they started.

The Boston club went back to 1876, the year the National League was born, and it had never missed a season since then. No wonder fans started at the headlines in disbelief. What did it mean, they asked themselves. Was this the beginning of a trend?

Yes, it was—as they soon found out. Within the next few years a succession of clubs from both major leagues moved from place to place like men on a checkerboard. Some owners moved because they could not make money where they were. Year after year they would end up losers. But some of the jumping club owners were doing well financially. If they thought they could make *more* money elsewhere, away they went. They gave little thought to the loyal and longtime fans they abandoned. What they did to baseball in New York is a striking example of their greed.

For 55 years New York City had three major league teams. The two National League clubs (Giants and Dodgers) played each other 22 times every year; their home grounds were in different boroughs of the city—Manhattan and Brooklyn. Because of these conditions, a real and intense rivalry flourished throughout the city. New York as a whole, was a "National League" city.

It is true, the New York Yankees were more successful at piling up world championships. But eventually they became a symbol of business—like efficiency, wealth, perfection and arrogance. A Yankee victory every year was taken for granted by New Yorkers. The Yankees were supposed to win—and they almost always did. "Rooting for them," said a sportswriter, "is like rooting for the U.S. Steel Company."

New York's heart belonged to the Dodgers and the Giants. It is not difficult, then, to imagine how New Yorkers felt when they learned that both clubs were going to California. They were stunned, and enraged at the money-seeking owners. In any event, the Big Town was left without a National League club, and the bottom dropped out of baseball enthusiasm.

It was disgraceful—the sports capital of America without a National League team. Mayor Robert F. Wagner decided that something had to be done. He appointed a committee of "prominent citizens" to find a replacement for the Dodgers and Giants. At the head of the committe was William A. Shea, an energetic lawyer and devoted sports fan. This happened in 1958, the year New York's two wandering clubs began playing in California as the Los Angeles Dodgers and the San Francisco Giants.

Bill Shea worked hard but he could not persuade any of the National League club owners to transfer to New York. He decided to form a new major league. One of its clubs would, of course, be in New York. He found wealthy backers in several cities who agreed to support his plan.

Then suddenly the two major leagues announced together that they were going to add two new clubs to each league—Los Angeles and Minneapolis to the American League, Houston and New York to the National League.

Shea quickly gave up his proposed league because he now had what he had wanted all along—a team for New York. He also had a backer for it, a person who had been one of his supporters.

She was Mrs. Charles Shipman Payson, an enthusiastic sportswoman and a rabid Giant fan from way back.

Mrs. Payson, a large, merry woman with light hair, was 57 years old in 1960, when she acquired New York's newest baseball team. She was born Joan Whitney, the sister of John Hay (Jock) Whitney, then Ambassador to Britain. They were co-owners of the famous Greentree Stable, which had produced a long string of fine race horses.

A friendly, easy-going person, Joan Payson was an all-around sports fan. Besides baseball and racing, she loved football, boxing, tennis, polo and rowing. (Her father, her husband and her brother had rowed at Yale.) Few men were as well informed on sports as she was.

Of all sports, she liked baseball best. And that, as it turned out, was most fortunate for baseball because what she did for the grand old game was one of the best things that ever happened to it.

That was a long way off, however. As things stood in 1960, all she had was a baseball club on paper. It had no players, no general manager, no field manager, no ball park, no equipment, no office, no minor league farm club, and no training quarters. It did not even have a name.

In the face of all this was her franchise contract with the National League. It stated that the new club must be put on the field at the start of the 1962 season. That was only a year and a half away.

First, the name of the club. The public was invited to vote on 10 names that had already been selected by the press as possibilities. About 1,000 letters were received. The top vote-

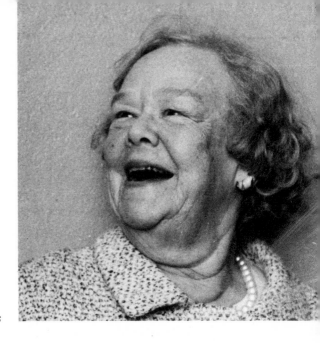

Joan Payson. *N.Y. Daily News*

getter was Mets (short for Metropolitans, the actual name of a New York major league team in the 1880's).

Joan Payson appointed one of her financial advisers, M. Donald Grant, president of the club.

George Weiss, the longtime general manager of the Yankees and recently retired by them (against his wishes) agreed to join the Mets. This was a stroke of luck. The Mets now had the best baseball brain in the country. Weiss was largely responsible for the continued success of the Yankees.

As for a ball park, New York City was about to build a big stadium where the Mets would play. But it wouldn't be finished in time for the 1962 season. Meanwhile the Mets arranged to use the vacant old Polo Grounds, where Joan Payson had watched the New York Giants as a schoolgirl.

Next, a field manager. Casey Stengel was the choice. The colorful, 71-year-old codger had been forcibly retired by the Yankees after winning 10 pennants for them in 12 years.

Casey was popular with the press. He was a comic. The baseball writers wrote pages about him, quoting the odd expressions and the twisted grammar he used. His special brand of English was called "Stengelese." The fans loved to read about him.

Casey was in his home in California when the Mets announced the big news in New York that he would manage the club. The writers rushed to the phones for a statement from Casey. He came through in style.

"It'll be great to be back in the Polar Grounds," he said. "It's a big honor for me to be joining the Knickerbockers." His acceptance speech was widely quoted in the press. Everybody laughed. "That's ole Case for you," they said. Instantly, he became the Mets' greatest asset.

By this time George Weiss had signed up several scouts, coaches, a front office staff, and was building a minor league system. The Mets were shaping up and were almost ready to go on the field—except for one thing. They had no team. They needed 25 players. Where would they come from?

The National League had the answer to that. It was covered in a new rule the league had just passed, designed to help the two new clubs and at the same time to fatten the bank rolls of the owners of the eight old clubs. This was the scheme:

Each of the eight old clubs would put 15 players into a pool. From this 120-man pool, which consisted mostly of bench warmers and castoffs, Houston and the Mets would each draw 16 players. They had to take two players, and two only, from each old club (at $75,000 apiece).

Then there would be another draw, this time at the high price of $125,00 a head for eight players—one from each old club. Each new club would get four more players this way, but at an outrageous cost.

The scheme was a holdup. The players the old clubs unloaded on the newcomers were mainly of low grade talent. They could not possibly compete with the established teams, as every informed person in baseball well knew. And they were costing the new clubs nearly $4,000,000—a sum that the eight owners would split among themselves.

Welcome to the National League, Houston and Mets!

Casey summed it up well when he sarcastically remarked: "I want to thank all those generous owners for giving us those great players they did not want."

The player draft took place in Cincinnati in October, 1961. A coin was tossed to decide which club would get the first choice in the $75,000 phase of the draft. Houston won the toss and chose Ed Bressoud, a San Francisco Giant infielder whose batting average was .211 that year.

The Mets first pick was Hobie Landrith, a part-time Giant catcher and pinch hitter. He batted .239 for the Giants in 1961.

A baseball scribe asked Casey why the Mets had picked Landrith for their Number One choice. "You gotta start with a catcher or you'll have all passed balls," replied Casey with a straight face.

The 16 $75,000 players and the four "premium players at $125,000 apiece that the Mets were forced to accept cost Joan Payson $1,700,000. Of this ragtag batch of 20 players, only three were proven major league regulars—and *they* were past their peak.

In the next few months George Weiss sold and traded several players, and collected a lot more of them from the majors and minors. By the time the Mets headed for their training quarters at St. Petersburg, Florida, he had formed a major league baseball operation in all its complex details.

The team, as everyone knew, was not going to be a winner. But at least it was a real team and it would be playing National League clubs.

In St. Petersburg the New York baseball writers immediately realized that the Mets were not going to go anywhere that season. They understood why and did not criticize the team in their stories. Instead, they wrote lively accounts that were full of good humor. They stressed the offbeat things that were happening, the human side of the players and the oddball utterances of Stengel, "the Old Perfessor," as they called him.

Their attitude was: "The Mets are bound to be losers, but who cares? Let's all have some fun out of it, no matter what."

No other baseball team had ever been handled by the press in such a lighthearted manner. New Yorkers loved to read the bright and colorful stories that were coming up from Florida almost daily. They became greatly interested in the club and could hardly wait for the season to open.

Old Dodger and Giant fans, who were once mortal enemies, found themselves back-slapping buddies rooting for the same team. And they had not yet seen it play. Their joy was unbound

New York went wild over the Mets before they ever played a game at home. Above, manager Casey Stengel leads the parade up Broadway. *N.Y. Daily News*

when the Mets beat the Yankees in the first meeting of the two teams. It was only a spring training exhibition game in Florida and did not really mean anything, but the Mets' new rooters in New York were grinning all over.

On the night of April 11, 1962, in St. Louis the Mets played their first official game. Casey chose Roger Craig to pitch the opener.

Craig was a 31-year-old ex-Dodger. The veteran hurler had cost the Mets $75,000 in the player draft. For that amount the Mets got a pitcher who, the year before, had won five games, lost six and had a frightful 6.15 earned run average.

Craig's performance against the Cardinals was brief and punishing. They hammered him for five runs in three innings. Casey then yanked him, thus giving Craig the distinction of being the first Met pitcher in history to be sent to the showers. Three other Met pitchers followed him to the mound as the Cards piled up an 11-to-4 victory.

The next day the Mets arrived in New York. The way the city greeted them you might think they had just won a world war for America. They were paraded up lower Broadway before cheering thousands. They were given a reception at City Hall and an official welcome by Mayor Wagner, who made a speech about the new ball park the city was building for them.

This made the Yankees boil over. After all, *they* were the World Champions. They had won more World Series and pennants than any other club. They had their own ball park and were faithful to New York. But they had never had a welcome parade up Broadway or a City Hall reception like the Mets got. It just wasn't fair.

Fair or not, the whole city was curious about the new ball club. The fans did not storm the Polo Grounds, however, when the Mets opened there on Friday the 13th of April. Only 12,000 of them showed up on that cold, raw day that produced a few snow flurries. (Casey still called the park the "Polar Grounds," and he was not far off this time.)

There had not been a major league game played in the Polo Grounds since September, 1957, when the Pirates beat the Giants. Now, almost five years later, it was the Pirates again. They beat the Mets, 4-3. The next day the Pirates won again, and on the following day, a Sunday they made it three straight against the Mets.

Oddly enough, the fans in the Polo Grounds were not at all downhearted by this string of losses. They cheered every time a Met came to bat, or threw a pitch, or hit a long ball whether it was caught or not. They encouraged every move the Met players made.

The Mets had now lost four straight, but that was no disgrace. They had been beaten by two established clubs of the highest rank. The Houston Colts were coming into the Polo Grounds next and the Mets would be playing someone their own size, another expansion team like themselves.

It was a tight game all the way. In the bottom of the ninth inning the Mets were trailing, 2-1, with two men out, when outfielder Gus Bell socked one into the stands, making the score, 2-2. The Mets had a chance to win the game in their half of the 10th when Felix Mantilla, their third baseman, doubled with one out. But on the next play, a grounder to deep short, Felix got caught between bases and was tagged out.

That was their last chance. In the top of the 11th with two Colts on base, up stepped Don Buddin, Houston's weakest hitter. He promptly hit a homer off Herb Moford. The Colts won, 5-2. (Don Buddin's batting average that season was .163; pitcher Herb Moford's entire record with the Mets was: won 0, lost 1.)

That was the club's fifth consecutive drubbing. The Cards were the next visitors to the Polo Grounds, for a two-game set on April 18 and 19. They wrapped up the pair of games with ease to the tune of 15 to 5 and 9 to 4. It was seven losses in a row now for the Mets, and the Pirates were next on their list.

The Mets went to Pittsburg and lost two more games. The season was just 11 days old and the Mets' record was now nine defeats, no victories. Already they were 9½ games out of first place because the Pirates, meanwhile, had won 10 straight. The Mets had tied a long-standing National League record: Most consecutive losses at start of season—9.

A benumbed and hopeless Casey sat in the dugout and said to a writer: "If we was losing like this in the middle of the season, nobody would notice. But we are losing at the beginning of the season and this sets up the possibility of losing 162 games, which would probably be an all-time record."

On Monday, April 23, the Mets broke the spell by beating the Pirates, 9-1. After the game they staged a champagne victory celebration in their dressing room.

Things got a little better for the Mets after that—but not for long. On the fifth of May their record was 16 losses, three victories.

By this time the club had set a pattern of play. It produced runs, more than four a game on an average. The Mets were rarely blanked. They were shut out only five times during the entire season. But they were allowing close to seven runs a game. This was because their pitching staff was terrible and their defense belonged in the Little League.

The outfielders let easy pop flies drop to the ground, untouched by human hands. They threw to the wrong bases; they lost balls in the sun.

The infield was a sieve. "They look like jugglers out there," said a fan as he watched shortstop Elio Chacon wrestle vainly with a ball that should have been on its way to second for a sure double play.

Old Met fans still talk about some of the historic wild throws they saw. Third baseman Frank Thomas in a game against the Cardinals fielded a routine grounder, then made the wildest throw in baseball history. It went 125 feet over the first baseman's head, according to restaurant owner Toots Shor. "Nobody ever done a thing like that," said Toots, who saw more than 100 games a year for some 50 years.

It could not have been much harder than the throw Chris Cannizzaro made one night in Los Angeles. Chris was catching when Maury Wills of the Dodgers beat out a bunt, then stole second. Chris was furious. Wills was taking his usual long lead off the base. Chris gave the pickoff signal. On the first pitch he threw to second—hard. So hard and high that it sailed over second base and was *caught on the fly* by Jim Hickman, the Mets' center fielder. Wills easily got to third on it and a moment later scored the winning run.

The infield had Casey dizzy. He was forever trying out new players and shifting others around the diamond. During the season he used eight first basemen, eight third basemen and 10 players at short and second base. None of the various combinations improved the club.

Worse still, were the catchers. Casey had three of them on his hands—Landrith, Cannizzaro and a rookie called Choo Choo Coleman. The trouble with them was that Landrith could catch but he couldn't throw; Cannizzaro could throw but he couldn't catch; Choo Choo could catch low pitches but the wasn't much good at anything else.

"Makes a man wonder," Casey mused one afternoon as he looked up and down the bench at his players. "Can't anybody here play this game?" His craggy face was gray with despair.

He had not seen anything yet. His Mets were on the brink of another long losing streak. It began in Houston on May 21.

At that time Joan Payson was in Greece on a long-planned trip with her children and friends. She had arranged to have cablegrams sent to her with the score of every game the Mets played. Daily the bad news came to her. It ran like this:

Lost to Houston, 2-3. Lost to Los Angeles, 8-17. Lost to San Francisco, 6-7, 10 innings.

It was monotonous—and depressing. Finally, she couldn't stand it any longer. She sent off a cablegram which said in essence: "Don't send scores any more when we lose; only when win." She was to have a long wait.

The losing streak stood at eight when the Mets returned to New York to play the Dodgers a double header on May 30. The "Amazin' Mets," as they were fondly called, drew an amazing crowd of 55,704. It was the largest crowd in the majors so far in 1962. They were on a downward path, deep in the cellar, in 10th place to stay. Yet more than 55,000 fans came out to root for them. There was no doubt now about the popularity of the new club.

The Dodgers demolished them in three straight games, then the Giants came into the Polo Grounds and swept four in a row. So, the Mets lost all seven games (for a total of 15 consecutive losses) but they played before huge crowds of howling fans

every day. No major league team had ever been supported
like that.

Who were these rabid fans and why were they so faithful
to a team they knew was hopeless? The writers tried to explain
it. They called the Met fans "The New Breed," a brand new
type of baseball fan.

First of all, the New Breed consisted of kids and teenagers
who were too young to have been Giant and Dodger fans, as
were their older brothers and fathers. These youngsters were
present at the birth of the Mets. They knew everything about
its early history and felt attached to it. This new club was their
very own and they adopted it.

(A quip making the rounds in New York at that time helps
explain this: "Why do you root for the Mets?" asks an oldtimer

of a teenager. "Because I've been a Met fan all my life," replies the youngster.)

Another segment of the New Breed were the uncountable thousands who cheered for the Mets because they were underdogs. The club was doomed from the beginning. The owners of the old clubs had arranged that. The Mets were playing against a stacked deck and this made the New Breed root harder than ever for them.

Finally, there were those who loved the Mets because they were so bad they were funny. The players tried hard and their morale was high. They got on well together and did not quarrel in the clubhouse. This is unusual in a losing club. But they could not win, and they managed to find so many new ways to lose, it all came out as high comedy.

Bill Veeck, former owner of the old St. Louis Browns, summed it all up when he said, "If you couldn't have any fun with the Mets, you couldn't have any fun any place. I'd love to follow them all summer."

On June 6 the Phillies took a doubleheader from the Mets and extended the clubs' losing streak to 17. Two days later Joan Payson got a cablegram. The Mets had at last won a game, the first of a doubleheader in Chicago. The Cubs took the second game, however.

The most popular player at this time was Marvin Throneberry. He came to the Mets from the Orioles in May. Casey used him as a pinch hitter for about a month, then put him on first as a regular.

Marv was a tall, amiable Tennessean, 28 years old. Almost immediately he became the favorite of the New Breed. They cheered him wildly, not because of his skills, which were sadly lacking, but because he could be counted on to do the unexpected. It was good natured cheering, not ridicule, and even Marv enjoyed it.

He booted routine grounders, circled awkwardly under pop flies and often dropped them. He muffed perfect pickoff throws to first. One time he caught a pickoff throw and had the baserunner out by a mile, but fell flat on his face as he lunged toward him.

For this miscue he did not get booed. The fans rewarded him by chanting: "Cranberry, Strawberry! We love Throneberry!" And they truly did. They called him "Marvelous Marv."

Five young fans regularly came to the games in white T-shirts. Each shirt had a different character painted on its back. When the five youngsters lined up in a row their backs spelled "M-A-R-V-!" Sometimes they spelled it backwards to encourage their idol: "V-R-A-M!"

One of Marv's best days at doing the unexpected was on June 17, when the Mets played Chicago at the Polo Grounds. In the first inning Don Landrum of the Cubs was caught in a rundown between first and second. In the middle of the action Marv found himself facing Landrum who was now trying to get back to first. But Marv did not have the ball. Instead of getting out of Landrum's way, Marv just stood there and Landrum ran into him (probably on purpose so that he could claim interference). Marv was the victim of an old trick. The umpire called it interference. So, instead of an out which would have ended the inning, the Cubs had a runner on first and two out. Quickly, they staged a four-run rally.

There was fire in Marv's eyes as he came to bat in the bottom of the first. Two men were on base and Marv was determined to make up for his bonehead play in the rundown.

Wham! He sent a screamer to the Mets' bullpen in right center. Marv took off like an Olympic sprinter. Head down and legs churning, he flew past first, rounded second and sped to third. He made the bag standing up. Two runs were in. He had cleaned the bases. The crowd yelled for Marv.

During the excitement Ernie Banks, the Cub's first baseman, quietly strolled over toward umpire Dusty Boggs, who was stationed near first. "He didn't step on the bag, Dusty. You saw it, didn't you?" The umpire nodded in agreement.

Banks went back to first and called for the ball. It was relayed to him. While this was going on, Marv was standing on third taking a deep breath. He glanced across the infield and saw to his horror that the umpire was calling him out at first.

The Mets did not protest the call. They knew Marv had missed the bag by a good two feet. What's more, he had done the same thing rounding second. Marv trotted to the dugout in silence.

Next up was Charley Neal, the Mets' second baseman. He drove the ball into the left field stands for a home run. As he started for first Casey waddled out of the dugout with his right arm extended. He pointed to first. Charley stepped on the bag. Casey then pointed to second and Charley stepped on that bag

The most popular player on the Mets worst team (1962) was Marvelous Marv Throneberry, shown here reaching in vain for a high throw from third. *N.Y. Daily News*

and kept going. Casey also pointed to third and to the plate. As Charley crossed it, scoring a run, Casey nodded in approval and went back to the dugout. The crowd cheered loudly.

The score was now 4-3 in the Cub's favor. If Marv had stepped on the bags it would have been 4-4. The Mets lost the game by one run. Marv made the last out in the game. In the ninth with two out and the tying run on first, he struck out.

The fans readily forgave Marv his sins on the field. He got more fan mail than any other player on the Mets. At the peak of the season he averaged about 100 letters a week.

His teammates liked him, as well as the fans. They thought of giving him a big cake on his birthday but decided not to. They were afraid he might drop it when it was handed to him.

The baseball writers delighted in recording the unusual records the Mets were piling up as they pursued their downward course. These were called "negative" statistics. The figures measured the misdeeds committed by a player or the club.

The Mets' nine-game losing streak at the start of the season was a negative statistic. Here are some other records:

Most wild pitches by staff in season—71; most home runs allowed in season—192; most double plays hit into in one game— 6; most batters hit by pitching staff—52; worst earned-run average for pitching staff—5.04; most errors committed by team—210. And so on.

Oddball, or meaningless, "silly" statistics, were also recorded by the writers. Examples: The Mets' three outfielders on opening day were fathers of 19 children, a record number for the majors.

Thursday was the jinx day for the Mets. The writers began to notice this after the club had lost nine straight games on Thursdays—and sure enough, the jinx continued all season. The Mets' Thursday record for 1962 was 0-15.

The Mets had two players with identical names, Bob Miller, pitcher, and Bob Miller, pitcher. This was recorded by the "silly" statistics keeper as a major-league record. R. G. Miller was a lefty; R. L. Miller threw right handed. Both hurlers enriched the Met record book with negative and silly statistics.

First, R. G. (Lefty) Miller: He had spent four years in the majors as a relief pitcher, but had retired from baseball in 1956 with a career record of 4-6. At age 27 in 1962, after a lapse of six years, he decided to try a comeback. He made it with the Mets. That's how badly they needed pitchers.

On July 24, 1962 in Milwaukee, Lefty was in the bullpen hoping to be summoned to the mound. He had yet to throw a ball for the club.

The Mets were locked in a 4-4 tie with the Braves. It was the bottom of the 12th and Del Crandall, Milwaukee's catcher, was at bat. He was hitting .297.

Casey waved to the bullpen for his new pitcher. Lefty strode to the mound and took his eight warmup pitches. Then he stared at the catcher's sign, went into his windup and put everything he had into his first pitch as a Met.

It was a slider. Crandall went for it. He blasted it into the left-field seats for a homer. Miller walked off the mound. The game was over. He had lost it, 5-4, with one pitch.

The negative statisticians loved that item. They decided that Lefty's performance was unique, that no other pitcher in the history of the majors had achieved such a feat in his first appearance with a club.

The other Miller (R. L.) also established some impressive statistics. He came to the Mets from the Cardinals with a 9-9 record as a relief pitcher for three seasons. He was one of the four $125,000 premium players the Mets took when the club was formed.

He was a hard thrower, a right hander, and a loser from the beginning. He lost his first game, then another and another. He deserved to lose most of them, but whenever he pitched a good game his teammates would blow it for him.

When he had lost 10 in a row the negative statisticians began to take notice of him. Maybe he's on his way to a record, they said. No pitcher had ever lost 13 games without winning at least one. It was late in the season but Miller still had time to pitch three more games.

Miller dropped the next two games. He had tied the worst pitching record. One more loss and he'd make it. The statisticians were on edge.

On the morning of September 29, the next to the last day

R. G. Miller and R. L. Miller with pitching arms extended. *N.Y. Daily News*

of the season, he was 0-12 and was scheduled to pitch that afternoon. The Mets were in Chicago.

Going into the seventh inning, the score was 1-1. The Mets came to bat. Outfielder Jim Hickman singled. Then Marvelous Marv sliced a two-bagger to left and Hickman scored all the way from first.

Miller made his 2-1 lead stand up. It was a precious victory for him—his first of the season (two days before October 1) and also his first complete game in two years.

His 1-12 winning percentage was .077. By coincidence, that figure was the exact batting average of Don Zimmer during his brief career with the Mets. Like Miller, Don was a $125,000 premium player. The infielder set a negative record by going hitless in 34 times at bat and was soon traded to Cincinnati.

Another $125,000 flop was pitcher Jay Hook who came to the Mets from Cincinnati with a five-year losing record. He continued to lose for the Mets. He was 8-19 for the season, and he allowed 137 earned runs, the most scored against a pitcher in the league.

However, two Met pitchers exceeded Hook's performance in the losing column. Al Jackson lost 20 games and Roger Craig led the league by losing 24.

And so the season ended with an avalanche of negative statistics. The Mets played all but two of their 162 games scheduled. They finished at the bottom, 60½ games out of first place, 18 games out of ninth.

They lost 120 games, won 40. No major league team in this century had lost that many games in one season. This established the Mets as without question the worst team of modern times and quite possibly of all time.*

There were a few cheerful notes, though. The club set an attendance record: Highest home attdenance by a last-place club —922,530.

They had established an identity and had won a following. They had made history. The best was yet to come. After all, they could not possibly get worse.

1963

Sure enough, they did improve in 1963—but not by much.

Marvelous Marv was sent back to the minors. Pitcher Roger Craig (5-22) replaced him as the fans' new non-hero. He responded by losing 18 straight games.

There were few bright spots that season, however. One was the exhibition game for charity the Mets played against the Yankees on June 20.

---

* Some baseball historians suggest that the Cleveland Spiders of 1899 might have been worse than the Mets. In the 12-club National League of that time, Cleveland lost 134 games and won 20. Home attendance dropped to near zero in August, as the club won only four of 30 games. It was forced to flee town in order to survive. The team played its remaining 35 games on the road and picked up a new nickname—the Cleveland Exiles. They lost all but one of the 35 road games.

A Met fan. *Linda Hirsch*

About 50,000 noisy Met fans carrying banners, placards, horns and bugles invaded Yankee Stadium for the game. Uniformed Yankee guards tried to tear down the banners and signs, but got nowhere.

The turmoil in the stands annoyed the World Champions. They considerd the game a meaningless nuisance, nothing to get excited about. Not so the Mets and their devoted followers. To them it was a World Series game in importance.

The game began when Jimmy Piersall, the Mets' new out-fielder, came to bat. A veteran of 12 years in the majors, Jimmy was noted for his hitting and his odd antics on the field.

He cracked out a double, got to third on a deep grounder and scored on a wild pitch. The Yankees tied the score in their half of the first.

In the third, Jimmy again led off with a hit. It was the first

87

of three more to come before the inning was over. The Yankees collapsed before the Mets' assault, which included singles by Hot Rod Kanehl and Tim Harkness, a double by Al Moran, a wild pitch and two walks. The rally put the Mets ahead, 6-1. The Yankees picked up one more run and the game ended, 6-2.

It was a great victory for Met fans and they celebrated it right then and there. They tore up their signs and scattered the bits on the field. They sang, cheered and waved hankerchiefs at the Yankee players as they ran for cover after the final out.

They had seen their team lose a total of 163 games while winning only 65 in less than a season and a half. But this one triumph over the World Champions made up for everything. And it proved to them what most National Leaguers have always said—that the Yankees were big winners only in an inferior league.

Three days after the victory Jimmy Piersall pulled one of his zany antics in a game at the Polo Grounds against the Phillies. He had a career record of 99 home runs at that time. He was anxious to reach 100 homers and vowed that when he did, he'd celebrate the event by running backward around the bases.

Jimmy sent one into the stands in the third inning and took off backwards for first. He kept on going that way and touched all the bags. "A born Met, a real nut," said some fans. But Casey was not amused. One comedian on the club (himself) was enough. Jimmy was soon traded to the Los Angeles Angels.

The Mets and the Phillies played the final ball game in the Polo Grounds on September 18. The old park was closed forever after that. The Mets would play in Shea Stadium next year.

Their 1963 season ended in Houston on September 29 with a 13-to-4 shellacking by Houston—the Mets' 111th defeat.

"We finished 20th," said Casey. "Tenth each year." It was a slight improvement, however, over the last season in games won and lost.

The big improvement was in attendance. The Mets, in last place, drew 1,080,108 fans, thus passing the million mark for the first time. Just across the Harlem River within sight of the shabby old Polo Grounds, the lordly Yankees in their vast stadium won their fourth straight pennant. They drew 1,308,920.

The Yankees were miles above the Mets in games won and lost (104-57 vs. 51-111) but not in attendance. In that race the Mets were almost even and were gaining rapidly.

1964

The Mets began their third season on the road with their usual defeat. This time it was to the Phillies who beat them twice. Then they came to New York for the grand opening of their sparkling new Shea Stadium. More than 50,000 Met rooters were there. (The day before, the Yankees had opened their season at home before a crowd of only 12,000.)

Joan Payson saw the opener from her box near the Met dugout and cheered heartily. But her presence did not inspire the Mets enough to win. They lost to the Pirates. The next day the Pirates won again. That made it four straight losses for the Mets.

The next day before 30,000 howling fans they whipped the Pirates, 6-0, to win their first game of the season.

"This team is twice as good as last year's," announced a baseball writer in the press box, who was noted for keeping useless statistics.

"How come?" he was asked by the scribe next to him.

"Well, last year's Mets lost eight in a row before winning their first game. This year's Mets got their first win after losing only four straight. They did it in half the amount of time it took the 1963 team. So, doesn't that make this team twice as good?"

Silly statistics like that appeared daily on the sports pages. The next one of note came to light on May 4, when the Mets played the Braves in Milwaukee.

It was a close game. The Braves were leading 2 to 1 in the top half of the ninth inning when Ron Hunt, the Mets' second baseman, made a dash for the plate on an infield grounder. But Ed Bailey, the Braves' big catcher, got the ball a split second before Ron went into his slide. As Ron shot across the plate he tried to knock the ball loose from Bailey. "Out!" bawled the umpire.

Immediately the two players were throwing punches at each

other. This triggered a free-for-all. Out of the dugout steamed Casey, intent on getting into the fray. The old man was just starting to swing when Denis Menke of the Braves grabbed him and pinned his arms from behind. He did not want to see Casey get hurt even though he was the opposing manager.

The statistic that emerged from this action was recorded as follows: Oldest man in a baseball uniform ever to get into a fight on a major league field—Casey Stengel, aged 73. (He was only two months away from his 74th birthday.)

Two days after the battle, the Mets played their 19th game of the season. They lost it and their record was 3-16. By coincidence, the original Mets had also been 3-16 after playing *their* 19th game two years ago. This was progress?

It was taken for granted that the 1964 Mets were destined for the cellar—and that is where they did finish. "In 30th place," as Casey would have it.

But they were never as bad as the original Mets, and they

(Opposite page) Casey at his 74th birthday celebration, clowning as usual. *N.Y. Daily News*

(Right) Ed Kranepool and his mom the day he became a Met. *N.Y. Daily News*

had lined up some young players who one day would bring sunshine to Shea.

They included outfielders Cleon Jones and Ron Swoboda, shortstop Bud Harrelson and first baseman Ed Kranepool.

The big surprise was the attendance at Shea Stadium. Despite the team's sorry record (53-109), it drew 1,732,594 fans. No last-place club had ever attracted that many people. For the first time, The Mets topped the Yankees in attendance. They outdrew the pennant-winners by more than 400,000.

1965

Would the Mets ever emerge from the cellar? It did not seem so as the 1965 season progressed. The pattern remained the same as before. For the fourth straight year, the Mets:

Were rated 100 to 1 against winning the flag.

Lost the opening game.

Did not reach the .500 mark at any time during the season.

Lost the final game.

Lost more than 100 games.

Finished last.

Set a new attendance record.

Among the other things the Mets lost was Casey Stengel.

After leaving his 75th birthday party at Toots Shor's restaurant, Casey slipped and fell on the sidewalk. He was taken to Roosevelt Hospital with a broken hip and spent three weeks there. Thereafter, he walked with the aid of a crooked black cane.

It would be impossible for him to manage the club, he said, because "I can't walk out to the mound to take the pitcher out with this here crooked cane."

Casey left for his home in California. On the way he stopped off in Kansas City, where he was born, to see his 78-year-old sister. She too, was recovering from a broken hip.

Wes Westrum, the old Giant catcher, replaced Casey as manager.

1966

Earnest and hard-working—quite the opposite of Casey—Wes finished the '65 season, then went on to '66. His first full season was his best.

It started off like every other season since the beginning. The Mets lost the opener. They lost it to the Braves in Shea Stadium, packed solid with 52,000 fans, and they lost it in typical Met fashion. They gave the game away.

Met pitcher Jack Fisher had a 2-1 lead in the ninth when Joe Torre, a .300 hitter, slammed one off the center field fence for a double. Then Lee Thomas singled to right field, where Cleon Jones picked up the ball and rifled it into the Braves' dugout beyond third. Torre scored, tying up the game, and Lee Thomas was on third.

Denis Menke came to bat and on the first pitch dropped a squeeze bunt to Jack Fisher on the mound. Thomas sped toward the plate. Fisher hurriedly threw to catcher Jerry Grote, but the ball went wide and Thomas scored. That did it. The game ended, 3-2.

But, to the delight of all Met fans, their team won the next day, 3 to 1, and on the following day the Mets came from behind in the ninth to post a 5-4 victory over the Braves.

The pair of wins produced a sparkling statistic. The Mets' record was now 2-1 and this meant that they were over the .500 mark for the first time in history. What did it matter if the season was only three days old?

Alas, the Mets dropped the next five games in a row and never got back to .500.

Westrum tried hard to instill a winning spirit in the Mets —and he partially succeeded. He told them that they weren't funny any more; the comic days were over. His fight talks didn't turn them into instant tigers, but they did show improvement.

Casey Stengel walking back from the pitcher's mound for the last time. *N.Y. Daily News*

During the month of July, they won 18 games and lost 14. It was a club record, their first winning month, and it put them in eighth place in the standings—the highest they had ever been in midseason.

They couldn't keep up the momentum, however. They faded in September, losing 25 of their last 35 games.

Still, the final figures were the best they had ever put together:

66 victories, the most ever.

95 defeats, the fewest ever and first time under 100.

1,932,693 attendance, the best ever (outdrew Yankees by more than 800,000).

Ninth place in the league, final standing, highest ever.

At last a National League club had finished beneath them. It was the Chicago Cubs (59-103), managed by Leo Durocher. He had left the Giants in 1955 after a falling out with owner Horace Stoneham and this was the first club he had managed since then.

Met fans were overjoyed at Leo's descent to the cellar. The old Giant fans among them had never forgiven Leo for having managed the Dodgers. And the old Dodger fans hated him for having jumped to the Giants.

And to add more frosting to the cake, the Mets finished higher than the Yankees, who now occupied the American League cellar for the first time in 54 years and suffered their lowest attendance in 21 years. The baseball battle for New York had clearly been won by the Mets.

1967

The fans who sat in Shea Stadium on Opening Day, 1967, were confident that their heroes would at last win the first game of the season. Numerology was on their side. In the beginning, the Mets had lost the first nine games. The next year they lost eight, then four, then two, and last year only one. The figures surely showed that their time had come as they faced the Pirates on that cold and raw afternoon before 32,000 shivering spectators.

But there was another set of numbers the forecasters had

overlooked. That was the number of errors the team made—four in eight innings. The Mets looked like a soccer team the way they kicked the ball around and presented the Pirates with three runs. Still, they managed to get three runs themselves. So the score was 3-3 when the Pirates came to bat in the ninth.

Shortstop Gene Alley opened the inning with a double. Then Jesse Gonder, who had caught for the Mets two years before, turned on his old team mates and hit another double, scoring Gene Alley.

That run was all the Pirates needed to win, but just to make sure they put two more across, thanks in part to two Met misplays—a passed ball and a wild throw by catcher Jerry Grote.

It was 6-3 when the Mets came up, and that was the final score. "Same old Mets," said the fans as they walked out of Shea shaking their heads.

They felt better about the Mets the next day, however, when they got their first look at Tom Seaver. He was the rookie pitcher the Mets had drawn out of a hat.

It happened this way. Tom was a pitcher on the University of California team in 1966 when he signed a contract with the Atlanta Braves for a $50,000 bonus. When Baseball Commissioner William D. Eckert was notified of this, he cancelled the contract. According to baseball law, the Braves should not have signed Tom until the college season was over. Tom did not know of this law. He had been assured by the Braves that everything was O.K.

The Commissioner ruled that the Braves must release Seaver, but any other club willing to pay the $50,000 bonus could claim him. Three clubs came forward—the Mets, the Cleveland Indians and the Phillies.

Tom was listening on the long distance phone in his home in Fresno, California, when the names of the three clubs were put in a hat in the Commissioner's office in New York. The Commissioner drew one name out of the hat. It was the Met's.

That is how the Mets, lucky at last, came up with a pitching gem who would soon make the fans forget the days of frustration they had so long endured.

Tom Seaver was born into an athletic family. Both of his

parents were fine amateur golfers. His father, Charles, Sr., was the Stanford University golf champion in 1932, and a member of America's Walker Cup team. He also played football and basketball at Stanford.

All of the four Seaver children were highly competitive among themselves and at the four different California universities they attended.

Tom's oldest sister, Katie, was a good volleyball player and swimmer at Stanford; Charles, Jr., swam on the University of California varsity; his sister, Carol, majored in physical education at UCLA; Tom went to USC on a baseball scholarship. He was the youngest of the brood and the most determined to succeed.

The Mets sent him to their farm club in Jacksonville, Florida in the spring of 1966. He posted a 12-12 record there and had an impressive strikeout mark of 188.

Tom was closely watched by the Met scouts and coaches. They liked what they saw. He was a "comer," they said, with great possibilities. He was an unusual pitcher; he liked to hit and field and he was fast on the bases.

The one word that persisted in all the reports sent back to New York was the noun "poise." Tom had natural poise, that all-important gift of remaining cool under pressure, unruffled, in control of oneself at all times.

He also had other attributes—a powerful build, coordination and a desire to improve his natural skills. He was just over six feet tall and weighed a solid 195 pounds when he came to the Mets in the spring of 1967.

With him from Jacksonville came Bud Harrelson, a skinny shortstop, also a kid second baseman named Ken Boswell. They came to stay.

On Opening Day in 1967, when the error-making Mets blew the game to Pittsburg (as described above), Tom sat on the bench and took it all in. He had never seen the Mets play before, not even on TV.

The next day he saw them play again. But this time he wasn't on the bench; he was on the mound.

Tom pitched well and showed great concentration, but he

Shortstop Bud Harrelson dives left and snares a hard drive. *Wide World*

began to tire in the sixth inning. He left the game in the seventh with a man on first. Chuck Estrada relieved him, got a double play, and the Mets went on to win, 3-2. Chuck got credit for the victory.

Tom's second start was also a winning game, but he needed help in that one, too. Not until his third start did he pitch his first complete game.

It took place in Chicago on April 25. Tom's fastball was hopping that day. He overpowered the Cubs with his speed and control. He allowed only four hits and kept them scoreless going into the bottom of the ninth. But the Mets had only a thin, 1-0 lead.

Tom faltered momentarily and walked the first man up. A sacrifice bunt moved the runner to second, but Tom got the next batter out.

With two men down, Tom was only one out away from a shutout victory. He then pitched to Ron Santo, the Cubs' third baseman, and made him bounce an easy grounder to Bud Harrelson at short. The game should have ended right then, but the ball kicked off Bud's glove and went into left field. The Cubs scored their first run on the error.

Instead of having a victory, Tom now had a tie game on his hands. He retired the next batter and ended the inning.

It was Tom's turn at bat at the start of the 10th. Manager Westrum thought of putting in a pinch hitter, but first asked Tom how he felt. "Fine," said Tom. Westrum let him bat for himself.

On the second pitch Tom singled to right. He was bunted to second, made third on a grounder and came home when outfielder Al Luplow rapped a single through the middle with two out.

Tom faced the Cubs in their half of the 10th. Cool and determined, he set them down, one-two-three, and walked off the field with a 2-1 victory.

It was a most significant game, for it displayed the handsome young pitcher's great assets—his poise and determination—and it affected the whole team.

Thereafter, the Mets seemed to play a little better behind Tom than they did behind other pitchers. His intense desire to win rubbed off on them.

The club continued to play well below the .500 mark and Tom had a hard time keeping his head above water. In late June he had a 5-4 record, when the club's was 23-40. The Mets were floundering in the cellar.

They were not hitting and were not giving the pitchers much support. Tom would win a game, then lose one, but he never let down, even when the Mets were hopelessly behind. In his drive to win, he did things on the field that few pitchers ever do.

For example, against the Braves he hit a single and two doubles, knocked in two runs and stole a base—though he lost, 4-3. In his next turn on the mound, he stole a base and beat the Dodgers. He beat the Reds, 7-3, and in this game he again displayed his exceptional poise.

In the sixth inning the Reds had runners on second and third, and no outs. Tom made Floyd Robinson pop up, then calmly struck out Vada Pinson and Pete Rose, both good hitters. This was typical of what he was doing for the Mets all season.

In early July he conquered the Giants and the Dodgers, and completed both games. His record was 8-5 on July 11, when the annual All-Star Game was played. The Mets were 31-47 and still 10th.

Tom Seaver, the great hurler, was a star from the start. He came to the Mets in 1967 and was named National League Rookie of the Year.

According to baseball law, every club in the majors must be represented by at least one player on the All-Star squads. This meant, of course, that a Met had to be chosen, but it did not necessarily mean that he'd get into the game.

All of the National League managers had seen Tom play and they picked him for the All-Star squad. He was the only Met chosen. He was deeply honored, but he did not expect to play. The All-Star pitching staff was loaded with topnotch veterans, such a Juan Marichal, Bob Gibson, Don Drysdale and Fergie Jenkins.

The game was played in the Angel's new stadium at Anaheim, California. It started at 4 o'clock, which meant that the game would be played in twilight. It was the worst time of day for visibility, especially for batters.

As a result, the best batters in the major leagues went down swinging, one after the other. In all, 30 men struck out during the long, extra-inning game.

The score was 1-1 in the top of the 15th, when Tony Perez of Cincinnati hit a homer and gave the National League a 2-1 lead. Tom was then warming up in the bull pen. Much to his surprise, manager Walt Alston summoned him and asked him to go in and protect the lead.

It was a tough assignment for a rookie pitcher with limited experience. But he was confident as he stood on the mound and faced the first batter, Tony Conigliaro. He made Tony fly out. The next man up was Carl Yastrzemski, the Red Sox slugger. Tom walked him. Next was Bill Freehan, who flied out. Then Tom struck out Ken Berry and the game was over.

His performance brought him acclaim and made him a celebrity in the world of sports. He was idolized in the press as no other Met had ever been.

"In personality, as well as in pitching ability, he had "winner" written all over him," wrote Leonard Koppett of the *New York Times*. "He was articulate, enthusiastic, funloving, but an instinctive leader. He liked to run bases, hit and field as well as pitch."

The Met fans at last had a real hero to root for. But all was not roses for Tom as the second half of the season got under way. After a month of ups and downs, his record was 10-8. But in mid-August he won two in a row, beating Atlanta, 6-1, and blanking the Pirates, 3-0.

That gave him 12 victories, only one short of the Met record of 13, which was set by Al Jackson back in 1963. (Al finished 13-17 that year.)

The next three weeks was agony for Tom as he sought his 13th win. Nothing went right for him. He made five tries and failed each time, but was charged with only two losses. His record dropped to 12-12.

Finally, on September 8 he got his 13th win when he beat the Reds, 5-4. Six days later he subdued the Braves with a four-hitter and beat them, 2-1. He was now officially the best pitcher in the history of the club—while still a rookie.

He was not yet through, though. Tom won two more games before the season ended. He finished, 16-13. This was a remarkable accomplishment in view of the Mets' sorry record. They lost 101 games and ended in 10th place. They had won 61 games. Tom had accounted for more than one-fourth of those victories.

He had set four club pitching records: most games won, 16; most complete games, 18; most strikeouts, 170; lowest earned run average, 2.76.

He was named National League Rookie of the Year by the baseball writers.

Just before the season ended Wes Westrum voluntarily resigned, admitting that the job was too much for him to handle.

1968

In the fall of 1967 the Mets announced that Gil Hodges would be their next manager. His name was familiar to all New York and Brooklyn fans. He had been the Dodgers' first baseman for many years, and he was one of the original Mets of 1962.

He left them the following year to manage the Washington Senators, who, like the Mets, were chronic cellar-dwellers. (They had finished at the bottom in five of the previous six years when Gil took them over.) In five years he brought them up from 10th place to sixth and made a name for himself as an excellent manager.

Gil was a large, broad-shouldered man of great physical strength. He spoke softly but his words carried authority. He was well-liked by his players, especially the younger ones who looked upon him as their father-figure.

One of them was Jerry Koosman, a left-handed pitcher the Mets acquired in a most unlikely way. It was the second time that sheer luck brought an outstanding pitcher into the Met fold.

This time they got their man on the recommendation of an usher in Shea Stadium. The usher's son, John Lucchese, was a catcher on an Army team at Fort Bliss, Texas, in 1964. Jerry Koosman, a lefthander, was the team's best pitcher. John wrote

New Met manager Gil
Hodges. N.Y. *Daily News*

his dad about Jerry, and his dad told the Mets. The Mets told
one of their scouts to take a look at Koosman.

A professional oddsmaker would probably give at least
10,000 to 1 that nothing would come of a tip like that, but in
this case he would have lost.

Jerry was a six-foot, three-inch, 205-pound farm boy from
Minnesota. He had a keen sense of humor and liked to tell how
he was "discovered."

"They sent a guy out to scout me," he recalled. "He offered
me $1,600 to sign. I turned him down, so the next time he
offered me $1,500. Every time he talked to me, he offered me
$100 less, and I finally signed for $1,200. I figured if I didn't
sign pretty soon, I'd end up owing the Mets money."

Jerry knocked about in the minors for three years. He came
up to the Mets in 1967 for a very brief appearance. He pitched
two games, lost both, and was sent to Jacksonville for more
seasoning.

He was back again in 1968, and Gil Hodges got his first
look at him in St.Petersburg. When spring training ended,
Hodges decided to let Jerry stay on.

When the Mets left Florida to start the regular season, they left behind them the worst spring training record the club had ever compiled—9-18. Hodges was not discouraged, however. "I think we'll win 70 games," he said.

The Mets had never won that many. Their best mark was 66 victories (in 1966); last year's total was 61. But Hodges saw some light in the Met cellar—a good pitching staff and the young players who should begin to surface.

The Opening Day jinx hovered over the Mets when they clashed with the Giants in San Francisco on April 10. Tom Seaver was on the mound opposing Juan Marichal, whose total record against the Mets was an unbelievable 17-1.

It was really a double jinx the Mets had to overcome—opening day plus the unbeatable Marichal. Was it possible? Yes—and it certainly looked that way from the start.

In the first inning Tommie Agee, the Mets' new center fielder, singled and stole second. Ron Swoboda rapped one through the middle and drove him home.

In the third, both Ken Boswell and Tommie Agee bounced singles through the infield, and then Ron smashed a homer into the left field seats. That gave Tom a 4-0 lead, and he was going well on the mound.

He slipped up only once, when he fed a home-run ball to Willie McCovey. It cost him two runs, but by the ninth he still had the lead, a comfortable 4-2. He needed only three more outs to bust the jinx forever.

Willie Mays, the first man up, lined a single off Ed Charles' glove at third. Willie McCovey, always dangerous, came up next but Tom made him pop up for the first out.

Mays got to second on a passed ball, and Jim Hart's single to left brought him home. That made it 4-3. Gil Hodges came out to the mound and removed Tom. He waved in Danny Frisella, a relief pitcher whose Met record was 1-6. Nate Oliver, the first batter to face Danny, promptly tagged him for a single. Hart moved to second. He was the tying run; Oliver at first, was the winning run.

Up came Jay Alou. He lined a double to the left field corner. Cleon Jones got the ball and whipped it to Bud Harrelson as Hart was rounding third. Bud wheeled and threw home to get Hart, but the ball went wide. Hart scored. Oliver, who had started running at the crack of the bat, kept right on running and made it all the way to the plate. The game was over. The Giants won, 5-4. The Mets had blown a four-run lead. The jinx remained unbroken.

They played like the Mets of old—but they were not that bad, and they knew it. No longer were they resigned to defeat. "We'll win tomorrow," they told each other. And they *did* win the next day, thanks in great part to Jerry Koosman.

In Los Angeles the next night, the 24-year-old rookie stifled the Dodgers with a four-hit shutout. The Mets won, 4-0.

Four days later the Mets were in New York for the opening game in Shea Stadium against the Giants. An afternoon crowd of 52,000 saw Jerry make his second start. Right away the young southpaw got himself in trouble.

Ron Hunt, the first Giant batter, singled. Jim Davenport poked a grounder to shortstop Al Weis for what should have been a double play. But Al booted the ball, and instead of two out, there were two men on base. Then Jerry walked Willie McCovey.

With the bases loaded and nobody out, Willie Mays came up. It looked like curtains for Jerry as he made his first pitch to Willie. It was a strike. So was his next pitch. He struck out Willie on four pitches. Jim Hart came up next. Koosman made him hit a high foul, which Jerry Grote caught just behind the plate. One more to go. It was Jack Hiatt, the Giants' catcher. He went down swinging before the southpaw's steaming deliveries.

Jerry got into no more trouble after his shaky start. He pitched eight more scoreless innings and gave the Mets a 3-0 victory.

A few days later in Shea, Jerry was on the mound against Houston. He allowed only four hits but gave up his first run of the season. The Mets won, 3-1.

Jerry had now won three games in a row; he had allowed only 15 hits and one run in 27 innings. He had struck out 24 batters and walked only seven.

Met fans were enraptured by the sensational hurler. By this

Met fans were noted for their loyalty to the team and the colorful signs and banners they displayed. Above, Banner Day at Shea Stadium. *Wide World Photos*

time, Jerry's name was known to millions of sports page addicts and television watchers.

"I haven't had this much fun since my third-grade picnic," beamed Jerry after his third victory. He then went out and made it four in a row by beating the Reds, 6-5. But he had to have help in this game in the last two innings. At any rate, he had tied a Met record by winning four straight.

Meantime, Tom Seaver was holding his own, although he had run into some hard luck. Nolan Ryan, another right-hander, was getting his share of victories, and so was the fourth starter, Dick Selma.

All four were stingy in yielding hits and runs and they

were getting good support in the field. By mid-June Koosman was 9-2, Selma 6-0, Ryan 5-4, and Seaver was 5-5. But Tom had a 1.89 earned run average and he was overdue for a run of good luck. He would surely improve his record.

The Mets, for the first time, had the best front-line pitching staff in the National League. And the four starters were surprisingly young. Koosman and Selma were 24; Seaver was 23, and Ryan was 21.

For all that, the Mets could not quite reach the .500 mark. They got within one victory of it three times in June, but could not make it. In July the gap began to widen. They were 49-54 on the 27th. Then they went into a sharp decline, losing 19 of the next 28 games. On August 24 they were 58-73 and in ninth place.

What had happened? They still had good pitching and their defense was holding up. Why weren't they up near the top? These were the questions asked by many dazed and disappointed fans.

The answer was easy. The Mets could not hit. They couldn't get their pitchers enough runs. They were at the bottom of the league in team batting average (.221 in midseason) and this weakness was just too much of a load for the pitchers to carry every day.

The Mets barely managed to escape the cellar. They finished ninth, just one game above Houston. They won 73 games (three more than Gil Hodges had predicted) and lost 89—the fewest they'd ever lost, and the most they'd ever won. It was the best showing of any Met team so far.

Jerry Koosman set a Met record by winning 19 games. He lost 12. Tom was 16-12, which was a shade better than his 16-13 of last year.

One of the highlights of the season was the Mets' showing in the All-Star Game. For the first time, more than one Met was chosen to play in the annual game. Three were picked: Tom, Koosman and Jerry Grote, who caught the first five innings. He did a good job in handling pitchers he had never caught before, but went hitless in two trips. The National League was leading, 1-0, when he left the game.

Tom pitched the seventh and eighth innings, and struck out five.

In the ninth inning, with nobody on base and two out, Jerry went in to face Carl Yastrzemski of the Red Sox. The National League was still leading, 1-0. Big Carl represented the tying run. Jerry struck him out.

Counting Tom's performance in last year's All-Star Game, Met pitchers had faced 12 American League All-Star batters and had struck out seven of them. The fans were impressed by the two young hurlers.

"These kids could win a World Series all by themselves—if they should ever play in one," commented one fan.

Fat chance! The odds against the Mets winning a pennant were —100 to 1 (and no takers) ever since they started back in 1962. And when they gathered in St. Petersburg in the spring of 1969, they were still a 100-to-1 shot in the preseason annual ratings of the Las Vegas oddsmakers.

1969

No matter what the odds were, they would never finish 10th again, or ninth. They could not do worse than to fall to sixth place because of the new setup in the majors.

In 1969 both leagues expanded from 10 clubs to 12, and each league was split into two six-team divisions—Eastern and Western. The Mets were in the Eastern Division and even if they finished in the cellar, they would only be in sixth place—if that was any comfort.

At the end of the season, the Eastern and Western divisional leaders of each league would meet in a set of best-of-five playoff games for the pennant. The two league champions, as before, would then meet in the traditional best-of-seven World Series.

Gil Hodges, who had suffered a heart attack just before the 1968 season ended, had recovered and was at the helm again in spring training.

His 1969 team was basically the same as last year's. He believed it would do much better because the players were more mature and more experienced. He looked for improvement in hitting and pitching.

One of the few rookies on the squad was Gary Gentry, a 23-year-old pitcher. He had a one-year college record of 17-1 at Arizona State and had spent two years in the minors.

"How many games do you think the club will win this year, Gil?" asked a reporter, remembering how close Hodges had been in his prediction last year.

"We should win 85," the manager replied. Many writers chuckled at the thought of the Mets winning that many. It meant an improvement of 12 games over last year's 73 victories.

As for the Eastern Division race, the Cards were the overwhelming favorites—and why not? They had won two pennants in a row and were as strong as ever. The Cubs might give them a good run, however, as Durocher now had a solid team. He had spent three years putting it together and was satisfied with it.

Montreal, the new expansion club, would be last. That left

the Mets, Phillies and Pirates to fight it out for third place, according to most forecasters.

Dick Young of the *New York Daily News* was the only baseball writer to pick the Mets to finish higher than third. He predicted they'd finish second—way behind the Cards, but a notch above the Cubs. Dick was scolded by his fellow writers for being too loyal to the Mets, his favorite team since the clownish days of Marvelous Marv. A gifted writer with a keen sense of humor, Dick had written scores of columns about his beloved Mets.

The Mets would surely break the opening day jinx this time, for their opponent would be Montreal. The Expos, of course, would be playing the first game of their career. What's more, they would be facing Tom Seaver in Shea Stadium before thousands of Met rooters. How could the Expos possibly win?

By walloping Tom Seaver and scoring on Ken Boswell's

errors, that's how. Both players were way off form that day. Before the Mets came to bat in the first inning the Expos had a 2-0 lead. Ken's boot of a grounder and Tom's pitching (a walk and a double by Bob Bailey) accounted for the two runs.

That was just the beginning of a three-and-a-half hour see-saw struggle during which Ken made three errors and Tom allowed four runs. One of them was a homer by pitcher Dan McGinn, his only one of the season.

Even so, the Mets fought back and took the lead. But they could not hold it. Going into the ninth, the Expos led, 11-6. The Mets staged a rally at this point. They scored four runs and had the tying run on second with two out, but Red Gaspar struck out and ended the game.

The Expos won, 11-10. Those 10 Met runs had been wasted. They represented a week's supply for the club. Was this a preview of the coming season, fans asked themselves as they filed out of the stadium.

They felt better when the Mets won the next two games against Montreal. But then the Cards came into Shea and took three straight from them. And so it went for the next month. The Mets would win a few and then they'd lose a few more.

On the morning of May 4, a Sunday, their record was 9-14. They were in fifth place, one game ahead of Montreal, and eight games behind the red-hot Cubs. They were in Chicago and had just lost two games to the Cubs. A Sunday doubleheader was scheduled for that afternoon.

Two more defeats at the hands of the Chicagoans would be a crusher. It might well mean that they were headed for permanent residence in the cellar, or near it.

But the Mets got up off the floor and came back strong. They erased the two Cub defeats with a pair of tough 3-2 games, won by Tom Seaver and Tug McGraw.

The double victory was important to the Mets. It convinced them that they could put a stop to those long losing streaks that had bled them to death in the past. And it showed them that they could hold their own against the Cubs.

The Mets did not know it at the time, but the pendulum was about to swing their way. They moved from fifth place to fourth in the division and were never lower than that from then on.

Slowly the Mets inched toward the .500 mark. Six weeks into the season, on May 21, Tom pitched a three-hitter and beat the Braves, 3-0. The victory brought the team's record to 18-18. It was the first time the Mets had ever reached .500 later than the opening week of the season.

The baseball writers turned out exultant stories about the great achievement, but the players didn't think it was much of anything. Actually, the mark meant nothing in the league standings.

"What's .500?" said Tom to a sportswriter. "Let's reach first place. That'll mean something. We're looking beyond .500."

They weren't looking very far the next day when the Braves bombed them, 15-3, and dropped them below .500. But that wasn't all. They lost the next four games, three of them to lowly Houston. That put them five under, at 18-23. They might never see .500 again, the way they were going.

g McGraw lets one fly.

"Now do you admit that .500 means something, Tom?" asked the sportswriter.

"I'm beginning to see what you mean," Tom smiled.

Then suddenly came the turnabout. The Mets toughened—and got some breaks. Playing in Shea Stadium, they edged San Diego, 1-0, in an 11-inning squeaker. The Giants came next and went down, one-two-three. After that three-game sweep, the Mets hit the Dodgers with a 2-1 victory.

They had now won five straight games, four of them by a one-run margin, and they were back at .500 (23-23). It felt great to be there.

There were two more games to be played at Shea before the Mets went on the road. They whipped the Dodgers, 5-2. Then, in a 15-inning struggle full of spectacular plays, they beat them again, this time, 1-0. The double sweep of the Giants and Dodgers brought their victory streak to seven.

The Amazin' Mets headed for California to play the same three teams on their home grounds. The Padres were the first victims. Rookie Gary Gentry set them down, 5-3, thus breaking a record for Met winning streaks. Eight in a row now. Jerry Koosman, who had been nursing a sore arm for a month, was back in form again. He took the second game, 4-1 striking out 11 Padres. The next day, Tom stood on the mound and struck out 14, winning, 3-2, for another clean sweep.

The Mets had now won 10 straight games and were rolling as never before. They were still hot two days later in San Francisco. They pummeled the Giants, 9-4, aided by the bats of Tommie Agee and Cleon Jones. Tommie blasted two homers into the seats, and Cleon also hit one out of sight.

Eleven straight now—but that was the end of the fabulous run. Giant pitcher Gaylord Perry beat them, 7-2, with a four-hitter.

The Mets shrugged off the setback. It did not bother them at all. Their self-confidence had soared to new heights during their long winning spree. They had risen to second place in the division, eight games behind the leading Cubs. Below them were the Cardinals, defending champions of the National League. The Cards had all but collapsed for reasons never made clear.

The Mets' great defensive outfield (left to right): Cleon Jones (lf), Tommie Agee (cf) and Ron Swoboda (rf). *N.Y. Daily News*

The fired-up Mets were churning with spirit and confidence. "The old Mets are dead," cried center fielder Tommie Agee. "We are the new Mets!" Tommie was' one the four key players who were mainly responsible for the team's exalted station. The others were Cleon Jones and the two pitching aces, Tom Seaver and Jerry Koosman.

Tommie Agee had flopped badly the previous year when he came to the Mets from the Chicago White Sox. He batted a meager .217 and hit only five homers for his new club. But this year he was a different man. His batting average rose to .271 and he hit 26 homers. Swift in the field and aggressive at the plate, Tommie was rated the best leadoff man in the majors. At the season's end, he received the National League's Comeback of the Year Award.

Cleon Jones swung a big bat for the Mets all season. Most of the time the left fielder was hitting around .350. He was a starter in the All-Star Game, along with Seaver and Koosman.

Behind it all was the cool and steady hand of Gil Hodges, the peerless leader. Few managers have ever been so admired as he was by the team he directed. Tom Seaver spoke for all of his teammates when he said:

"When everyone else got excited, when we were scrambling to catch the Cubs, Gil remained calm. The tenser the situation, the more he concentrated. He never wavered, never came within a mile of panic, always observing, always maneuvering, always thinking."

The only time Gil lost his cool was in a doubleheader on July 30, when the Mets were taking a terrible pasting from Houston in Shea Stadium. The Astros had won the first game, 16-3, with a record-breaking pair of grand-slam homers in the 11th inning. Now they were on their way to another lopsided victory, with a 10-run third inning, when Gil suddenly emerged from the dugout.

He walked slowly toward the mound. Everyone thought that he was about to make a routine pitching change, but he wasn't. When he got to the mound, he didn't stop. He kept on walking all the way to left field, where he spoke briefly to Cleon Jones. Then Gil turned and headed back to the dugout. A few steps behind him walking with head down was Cleon. Hodges was taking him out of the game because he felt that Cleon had loafed on a hit into the left field corner.

Gil later announced that "Cleon's leg was bothering him," but everyone in Shea knew it was a disciplinary move. The lesson was lost on no one. The team got the message: You played all out for Hodges, or you didn't play at all. The fact that Cleon was an All-Star and a contender for the league batting championship, made no difference.

The day after the double drubbing while Cleon sat on the bench, Houston did it again. Tom Griffin, the Astros' rookie pitcher, shut the Mets out with four hits and won, 2-0.

The battered Mets went on the road after that loss to play three Western Division clubs—Cincinnati, Atlanta and Houston.

114

They split even against the Reds and Braves, then came into the Astrodome for a three-game series.

The Mets were thirsting for revenge. The Astros were a weak club, floundering in fifth place in their division and never a contender for the title. They should be easy for the Mets, but for some reason the Astros seemed to have the Indian sign on the New Yorkers. The two clubs had met nine times so far and the Astros had won seven games. This would be the Mets' last chance to get back some of those lost games.

Alas, it was a disaster for them. They lost all three games. The Astros had now won 10 of the 12 games they had played each other.

Dazed, the Mets headed for home. It was August 15 and they were in third place, nine and a half games behind the Cubs and only three and a half ahead of Pittsburg. They would have to go some to save third place. They had 49 games to play.

Gil Hodges had often told his players that they had more bounce-back ability than any team he had ever seen. And that is what he told them again as they got ready to take on San Diego in New York. It was to be a four-game series—two double-headers in two days.

The Mets knew that if they were going to bounce back, they had to do it right away. The Padres were the weakest club in the league and time was running short.

The Mets swept both doubleheaders by the scores of 2-0, 2-1, 3-2, and 3-2. They squeaked through by the narrowest of margins, but it put them back in second place—and they were off and running.

Now they were eight games behind the Cubs with 42 to play.

The Giants were next. The Mets took two games from them, but dropped the third. Then they faced the Dodgers and swept a three-game series from them again.

Meanwhile the Cubs had gone through a losing week, and suddenly the Mets found themselves in the pennant race. They were only five games behind the Cubs now and there were 39 more to play.

"Once more, I felt we were going to make it," Tom Seaver later recalled. "The Cubs were panicking, and we weren't."

On to San Diego went the Mets on their last swing to the West Coast. They opened with a doubleheader. Tom Seaver gave up two homers in the first game, but the Mets got eight runs for him and won, 8-4. Jim McAndrew blanked the Padres in the second game, 3-0, and the next day Jerry Koosman produced a two-hitter and won, 4-1.

Another sweep. The Mets were steaming. They had played 13 games in the last 11 days and had lost only one. But they could not keep up the torrid pace forever. Against the Giants and the Dodgers they lost four games and won three, but were not seriously damaged. The Cubs weren't doing too well, either.

Heading back to New York on September 4, the slightly battered Mets were still five games behind the Cubs. The Cardinals had plunged to oblivion. The race was between the Mets and the Cubs. They would meet in Shea Stadium on September 8 and 9, and this could well be the showdown.

But first, the Mets would entertain the Phillies in Shea, in a four-game series starting on September 5, a Friday. On the same day, the Cubs would be playing the Pirates in Chicago.

Before a huge crowd, Seaver started against the Phillies in the first game of the twi-night doubleheader. Before he made his first pitch, the scoreboard flashed the happy news that the Pirates had beaten the Cubs.

Tom was in his usual good form. He hurled a five-hitter and won, 5-1. It was his 20th victory and a record high for a Met pitcher. But the Phillies put a damper on an almost perfect evening for the Mets by winning the second game, 4-2.

The next day was bright and sunny for the Mets, as Tug McGraw and Don Cardwell combined on a six-hit, 3-0 victory. While the game was going on, the scoreboard danced with figures, showing that Pittsburg had flattened the Cubs, 13-4.

On Sunday, the following day, the scoreboard went wild while the Mets wrapped up their final game with the Phillies with a 9-3 win. Fans in Shea alternately cheered and groaned as the board showed the Cubs behind, 4-2; then ahead 5-4; then even, 5-5, in the ninth and 10th innings. In the 11th the Cubs finally succumbed, 6-5.

It was more than the scoreboard watchers could stand. They

could not wait for tomorrow. The Cubs were coming to town. Leo Durocher would be with them—Leo the Lip, who couldn't take defeat and was ordering his pitchers to throw beanballs to intimidate opposing batters.

The whole city buzzed with excitement that night. It was gripped in a pennant fever, the likes of which had not been felt since the glory days of the old Giants and Dodgers years ago. For all their pennants, the Yankees had never stirred the town like this.

The Cubs came into Shea leading by two and a half games. If they lost both games they would still be in front, but only by half a game—and they'd be reeling like a fighter backed up against the ropes.

Suppose the Cubs won both games. That could swamp the Mets, for they would hardly have time to make up a four and a half game deficit.

But that couldn't possibly happen, insisted the faithful Met statisticians, because—well, look at the figures: The Cubs had lost 10 of their last 18 games; the Mets had lost only six of their last 24 games. The Mets were hot; the Cubs were in a tailspin. Furthermore, the Mets would have their two aces going for them, Seaver and Koosman, and on their home grounds.

It was Jerry Koosman against Bill Hands, the Cubs' 20-game winner. The big series was on. Jerry made Don Kessinger, the Cubs' leadoff man, fly out. Then he struck out the next two men.

Tommie Agee, leading off for the Mets, stepped up to the plate. The first pitch Hands threw was a high fast one, close to Tommie's head. It sent him sprawling into the dirt. It was an intimidating pitch, no doubt about it. Durocher was at it again, ordering the beanball from the dugout. The Mets went down in order.

Every true baseball fan in the park knew what was coming when Jerry took the mound in the second and faced Ron Santo, the Cub captain. Jerry's first pitch hit Santo hard, on the elbow. It was a painful blow.

It did not trigger a battle, however. Both dugouts were quiet as Santo went to first rubbing his elbow. Santo and Jerry did not exchange any words. They did not even look at each other.

But the message was clear: Met pitchers would protect their batters if Club pitchers threw at them. And that was the end of the "beanball war." Jerry struck out three batters in a row and sauntered back to the dugout.

Bud Harrelson's single in the bottom of the third was the first hit of the game. Jerry tried to bunt him to second, but popped up. Then Tommie Agee came to bat.

In the press box the writers were talking about the beanball and how it can work either of two ways. It can scare a batter and subdue him, or it can make him angry and more dangerous than ever. What would Tommie do?

He gave the writers the answer they were looking for. Tommie hit a homer on the first pitch and put the Mets ahead, 2-0.

The Cubs got to Jerry in the sixth with a barrage of three singles in a row. One run came in and the tying run was on third. Ron Santo flied out, but deep enough to bring in the tying run.

The Mets wasted no time in breaking the 2-2 tie in their half of the sixth. Tommie Agee, still smouldering, ripped a double down the third base line. Then rookie Ron Garret, a .218 hitter, rifled a single through the right side. Tommie took off and went all the way. He scored in a close play at home. The Mets were in front again, 3-2.

And that's how the game ended, after Jerry cooly fanned three Cubs in a row in the ninth, for a total of 13 strikeouts.

The following night a confident Tom Seaver swept through the first nine batters while his teammates shelled Fergie Jenkins, the Cubs' best pitcher, for four runs.

Tom gave up three hits and a run in the fourth. But in the Met half of the inning he doubled and scored a run. As he crossed the plate 58,000 fans broke out in song. "Goodbye, Leo," they caroled to Durocher and waved their handkerchiefs at him. Leo sat on the bench in gloomy silence. For once, his lip was not flapping. The mass sing-along continued throughout the game.

After the fourth, Tom held the Cubs at bay and coasted through to a 7-to-1 victory. It was a sweet one, especially for Joan Payson who sat beaming in her box next to the Met dugout.

Jerry Koosman, southpaw ace, with Joan Payson, Mets owner and newly elected president. N.Y. *Daily News*

She had recently been made president of the club which she owned.

The Cubs departed for Philadelphia, their once-proud lead of nine and a half games down to a meager half. The Met victory was their sixth straight loss.

The Mets remained in Shea to take on the Expos in a twinight double-header the next day, Monday, September 10. If they could win both games they would be in first place no matter what the Cubs did in Philadelphia.

It is doubtful if anyone who sat in Shea Stadium that

119

Monday night will ever forget it. Fans were drained of emotion as they watched the tough, extra-inning struggle on the field before them, and at the same time followed the scoreboard's account of another seesaw battle that was going on in Philadelphia.

For some three hours the lead kept shifting in both games. Victory or defeat could come quickly at any moment to any of the four teams engaged.

Finally, the end came in New York. The teams were deadlocked at 2-2, when the Mets came to bat in the 12th inning. Expo pitcher Bill Stoneman got two quick putouts and it looked as if the game would go into another inning at least. But Cleon Jones sent a blooper to left, and Rod Gaspar walked on four straight pitches. The crowd was standing now and giving forth with a nonstop roar.

Up came Ken Boswell, the Mets' second baseman. He was on a wild hitting streak, batting close to .450. Ken rapped a sharp grounder through the box into center field and Cleon came home standing up with the winning run. The game was over. The Mets had won, 3-2. It was 8:43 P.M.

The Mets were in first place. The aisles were jammed with people dancing and cavorting. Thousands stood on their feet and yelled happily.

"Look," said a fan. "The President of the Mets is crying." He pointed to Joan Payson in her box. She was wiping tears from her eyes.

For 155 consecutive days, the Cubs had been in first place —every day since the season started. Now the Mets were there.

But wait a minute! Were they *really* first? Yes, the Mets were a few percentage points ahead of the Cubs, but the game in Philadelphia was not over yet. It was dragging along at 2-2 and if the Cubs won it, they would be back in first again.

By this time, the second game in New York had started. A new set of figures popped up on the scoreboard: the Cubs were trailing, 3-2, in the seventh inning.

It was the third inning in New York. The scoreboard flash ignited the Mets. They exploded with a five-run rally and went ahead, 6-1. The frenzied crowd in Shea was almost out of control.

120

The Mets were sure to take the second game—and look at the scoreboard now! It showed the Phillies scoring three more runs in the eighth. The Mets would sleep in first place that night.

It became official at 11:30 P.M. when both games were completed. The Cubs had lost, 6-2, and the Mets had won, 7-1, and were firmly in first place.

Now the question was, could they hold the lead? The answer to that was not long in coming. They not only held it, they suddenly turned the pennant race into a shambles. The Cubs caved in and the Mets could do no wrong.

They took another game from Montreal (while the Cubs were losing another one to the Phillies). Then they journeyed to Pittsburg to take on the hottest hitting team in baseball on its home grounds.

The series started with a twi-night doubleheader, and when it was over the press box sat stunned, the statisticians were gasping, and the Mets were in heaven. Here is what happened:

In the first game, Don Cardwell pitched a 1-0 shutout and knocked in his own winning run. In the second game, Jerry

Second baseman Ken Boswell hit the run that put the Mets in first place.

Hundreds of fans swarmed onto the field when the Mets won the Eastern Division title by beating the Cards 6-0 in Shea on September 24, 1969. *N.Y. Daily News*

Koosman also pitched a 1-0 shutout and also knocked in his own winning run.

Nothing like that had ever happened before. "Two one-to-nothing games, with both runs driven in by the pitchers!" gasped Tom Seaver. "How can we lose after that?"

On September 24, in the middle of a nine-game winning streak, the Mets clinched the Eastern Division championship by beating the Cards, 6-0, in Shea Stadium.

The big scoreboard flashed: LOOK WHO'S NUMBER ONE NOW.... NOT THE CUBS NOR THE CARDS ... ONLY THE AMAZING METS."

Whereupon hundreds of young fanatics surged from their seats and swarmed on to the field. They ripped up the sod and brought it home for souvenirs. They stole all the bases and the home plate. They took everything that could be pried loose.

A week later the season ended. The Mets finished with a 100-62 record, eight games ahead of the second-place Cubs. They had the best won-lost record in the National League. They had ended a seven-year drought and were now supreme.

122

However, as the players well knew, they really hadn't won anything yet. They had not won the pennant. True, they had finished first in their division, but they did not get a flag or a trophy for that. What they did get was the right to play a three-out-of-five series against the Western divisional leader for the championship of the league.

The Atlanta Braves won the National League's Western Division with a 93-69 record. The Mets would play them for the pennant. Meanwhile, Baltimore and Minnesota, the divisional winners in the American League, would meet for the championship of their league.

The playoffs in both leagues were scheduled to start on the same day, October 4, a Saturday. The Orioles and the Twins would play in Baltimore at 1 o'clock. Three hours later in Atlanta, the Mets and the Braves would start their first game.

The different starting times enabled millions of TV viewers to see two ball games, one after the other, and have six solid hours of baseball. And if they were so inclined, they could have six more hours of it the next day, as the same schedule would prevail.

For once, the Mets were the favorites. They had won eight games out of 12 from the Braves during the regular season, and Tom Seaver had beaten them three times in his three starts against them. He would pitch the opener.

Tom was then reaching the peak of his career. He was the "winningest" pitcher in the major leagues with his dazzling 25-7 record. He had finished the season strong, winning his last 10 games in a row.

The Mets were confident of victory. Many players brought their wives to Atlanta. Tom's wife, Nancy, was there. Casey Stengel was on hand. So was Joan Payson. She made her entrance in a golf cart from right field to her box behind third. The Met family was in a festive mood.

Tom's opponent was Phil Niekro, a knuckle-ball specialist who had won 23 games for the Braves, but was 0-3 against the Mets during the season.

The fans expected a tight pitchers' duel, but the game did not turn out that way. Both pitchers were off form and neither finished.

The Mets got two runs in the second inning, one of them on a wild pitch, but Atlanta picked up a run in their half of the second and got two more in the third. This put the Braves ahead, 3-2 Tom was tagged for four doubles and a single in the first three innings. The Mets took the lead in the fourth when Harrelson laced a two-run triple down the first base line. In the fifth, Atlanta's Tony Gonzalez homered off Tom, tying the score at 4-4. The tie lasted until the seventh when Hank Aaron drove one into the left-field seats and put the Braves in front, 5-4.

Things looked dark for the Mets. Tom had failed them. He had given up five runs (all earned) on eight hits, had walked three and struck out only two. As the Mets came to bat in the eighth, Niekro needed just six outs and the game would be his.

But the Mets suddenly woke up. Wayne Garrett, a rookie utility infielder, opened the inning by driving a double past Clete Boyer at third. Then Cleon Jones lifted a single to left field and Garrett came home. It was a new ball game, 5-5.

Next up was Art Shamsky. He singled to left and Cleon moved to second. Then came a series of breaks for the Mets. Cleon got to third on a botched pickoff play by catcher Bob Didier. Kranepool poked a slow grounder toward Orlando Cepeda at first. Cepeda raced in for it to nail Cleon at the plate, but his throw to Didier was wild, and Cleon scored. Once more the Mets took the lead, 6-5.

With two out and two men on base, Bud Harrelson came up. Niekro purposely walked him to get at Seaver, who was coming up next. But Gil Hodges sent in J.C. Martin to pinch hit for Tom. Martin was a utility infielder with a .209 batting average. On the first pitch he lined a clean single to center field and the ball bounced through Tony Gonzalez. It was a costly error. By the time he got the ball three runs were in and Martin was on his way to third. He was thrown out, but the Mets now had a 9-5 lead. Four of the five Met runs in the wild inning were unearned.

Ron Taylor, the relief pitcher for Tom, held the Braves scoreless in the eighth and ninth. And so ended the National League's first divisional playoff game in its 94 years of existence.

In the American League, the Orioles squeezed out a 4-3

victory over the Twins in a 12-inning marathon in Baltimore.

The next day in Atlanta, the Amazing Mets did it again. Exuding more confidence than ever, they bombed the Braves with homers by Tommie Agee, Ken Boswell and Cleon Jones among the 13 hits they got from a parade of six Atlanta pitchers.

Jerry Koosman was staked to leads of 8-0 and 9-1, and looked unbeatable. But suddenly, with two out in the fifth, he came apart at the seams. Two walks, a single, a double and a three-run homer by Hank Aaron accounted for five runs. That was all for Jerry.

Except for that one frantic inning, it was no contest. The Mets won, 11-6, while up in Baltimore the Orioles also made it two in a row by beating the Twins, 1-0, on Dave McNally's three-hitter.

Wayne Garrett on the brink of a double.

The next day, Monday, October 6, the Mets were back in New York. All they had to do now was to win one game to clinch the pennant. They could wrap it up that very afternoon and have a four-day rest before the World Series began.

Gary Gentry, the Mets' starter who was celebrating his 23rd birthday, was in trouble right away. He got only one man out before Hank Aaron's two-run homer put him behind. Gary got through the second inning, but in the third he was on the brink of disaster again. With none out, Gonzales tagged him for a single, then Aaron doubled and Rico Carty hit a long drive into the left-field stands. It was a foul by inches.

Gil Hodges waited no longer. Out came Gary, his birthday spoiled, and in came Nolan Ryan. With a brilliant display of pitching under pressure, Nolan whiffed Carty and Boyer, and got Didier out on a soft fly.

Tommie Agee's home run in the third and Ken Boswell's two-run homer in the fourth put the Mets ahead, 3-2. The hard-throwing Ryan made his only mistake in the fifth, when he grooved a two-run homer pitch to Cepeda that gave the Braves a 4-3 lead.

But it lasted only until the Mets came to bat in that inning. Ryan himself led off with a single, then Wayne Garrett lined a homer into the right-field bullpen.

The Mets now led, 5-4, and from then on a roaring, standing- room crowd of 53,193 delirious fans kept chanting "We want more! We want more!"

The Mets gave them more: one more run in the fifth and another one in the sixth, while Ryan held the Braves in check. It was his day. He allowed only three hits in the seven innings he pitched; he walked two and fanned seven, got two hits and scored two runs. The final score was Mets 7, Braves 4.

It was official. The Mets had won the National League pennant. It was incredible. The Mets themselves could hardly believe it.

"Last spring in training camp, I don't think there was a guy on the club who thought we'd win this thing—and I mean Gil Hodges, too" said Ken Boswell.

The happy Mets win the pennant and swarm around Nolan Ryan (30), winning pitcher, after their sweep over the Atlanta Braves on October 6. N.Y. *Daily News*

Now for the World Series. The Mets would go against the tough and capable Orioles, who had strangled the Twins, 11-2, in the third playoff game.

The oddsmakers installed them as the 9-to-5 favorites to win the Series, and with good reason: they were the winningest club in the majors (109-53); they had made a shambles of their division by finishing 19 games in front of the pack; their regular lineup was considered the "strongest ever," superior to the 1966 Orioles, who had demolished the Dodgers in four straight Series games.

As for the Mets' three front-line pitchers—Seaver, Koosman and Gentry—well, they could be hit, said the Orioles. They didn't look so good in the playoffs. All three got roughed up and couldn't finish.

"They say the Mets have desire," said Oriole manager Earl Weaver to a reporter just before the game began. "Well, the Orioles have just as much desire—and a lot more talent."

Saturday, October 11, was a mild and sunny day in Baltimore when the teams came together in Memorial Stadium.

Mike Cuellar, a screwball specialist and a 23-game winner for Baltimore, started the game. He got Agee and Harrelson to ground out to Brooks Robinson at third. Cleon Jones tagged him for a single, but died on first as Donn Clendenon struck out. (Clendenon, who came to the Mets in midseason, shared first base with Ed Kranepool and was also used as a pinch hitter.)

Left fielders Don Buford, leading off for the Orioles, looked at Tom Seaver's first pitch and let it go. It was a ball. Tom wound up and sent across his fast one. *Bong!* Buford lofted it over the bullpen gate in right field. Tom got out of the inning without further damage, except for Boog Powell's single with two out.

The score was still 1-0 when the O's came up in the fourth. Tom disposed of Boog Powell, the gigantic first baseman, and Brooks Robinson, rated the best third baseman in the majors. Then catcher "Ellie" Hendricks, sixth in the lineup and a .244 hitter, singled through the right side.

Tom's control was off and he was heading for trouble. He walked Dave Johnson; then Mark Belanger lined to right.

Hendricks scored, and it was 2-0. Mike Cuellar, a .117 hitter, looped a single into short left, scoring Johnson. Now it was 3-0. Don Buford promptly belted a double against the right-field wall, and it was 4-0. Tom finally got the third out when Paul Blair grounded to Ed Charles at third.

Cuellar coasted along in full command, but gave up a run in the seventh on two singles and a walk. Brooks Robinson stifled a Met rally in that inning by making a barehanded grab of a tantalizing dribbler and, in one fluid motion, firing the ball to first in time to get Rod Gaspar. The magnificent play momentarily stunned the crowd; then came a thunderous roar as the first-base umpire flashed the "out" signal.

There was no more scoring. The game ended, 4-1, a crushing defeat for the Mets. They well knew that the first game in any World Series is vitally important. Could they stage a comeback?

Arthur Daley, sports columnist for the New York Times didn't think so. He wrote in his column the next day: "They [the O's] punctured a bubble. They shattered the Met mystique. They won with superior pitching, superior hitting and superior fielding. What made it seem particularly shattering is that the Baltimores may never again in this Series have to look nervously back, listening for footsteps behind them."

Forecaster Daley saw the Orioles in front all the way. So did the oddsmakers. They made them the 4-to-1 favorites.

The sceond game was a battle of the southpaws—Jerry Koosman, the Mets' clutch pitcher during the pennant drive, against veteran Dave McNally (20-7) who had blanked the Twins with a three-hitter just a week ago.

It was Columbus Day and also the second birthday of Michael Scott Koosman, Jerry's son, who was not in the stands to see his old man pitch one of the best games of his career.

Dave McNally was also in great form and did not yield a hit until the third, when Al Weis singled to center. He did not score, however. But in the next inning, Donn Clendenon led off with a home run over the right-field fence, and the Mets were ahead for the first time in the Series.

Meanwhile Jerry was pitching flawlessly, baffling the O's with his blazing deliveries and control. They could not hit him. The only Oriole who got on base in the first six innings was Dave Johnson, who walked in the second.

Jerry went into the seventh inning with a no-hitter going, but Paul Blair spoiled it for him with a clean single to the left side. With two out, Blair stole second and Brooks Robinson brought him home with a single through the box. The score was 1-1.

Both sides went down in order in the eighth. At the start of the ninth in this tense pitcher's duel, McNally had allowed only three hits, and Koosman but two.

McNally fanned Clendenon, and Swoboda grounded out. But Ed Charles laced a single past Brooks Robinson, and in a daring hit-and-run play Grote sent him to third on a single to the left side.

Next up was Al Weis. He had singled in the third, fanned in the fifth and was walked in the seventh. Manager Earl Weaver decided against walking Weis this time, (Koosman was up next) as he was such a weak hitter—.215 for the season. On his first pitch, Weis ripped a high slider to left field, scoring Charles.

For the second time in the game Jerry had a one-run lead. He seemed certain to hold it, as he retired Don Buford on an outfield fly and Paul Blair on a grounder to short.

But Jerry abruptly lost his touch, and what happened next was enough to give the Met bench heart failure, to say nothing of the hundreds of New York rooters in Memorial Stadium. Jerry walked Frank Robinson on a 3-and-two pitch, and then walked Boog Powell, also on a full count. With the always-dangerous Brooks Robinson coming up, Gil Hodges decided that Jerry had gone far enough.

Ron Taylor, who had stopped the O's in two relief innings in the opener, was given the task of smothering the threat. Taylor fell behind to Brooks, three balls and one strike. Brooks fouled off a pitch, and now it was a full count. Then Brooks bounced to Ed Charles at third. Ed took a step toward the bag, intending to tag it for a forceout, but he instantly realized that the runner had him beaten. Quickly he turned and fired the ball to first. Clendenon had to dig it out of the dirt, but he got it just in time to beat Brooks by half a step for the final out. The Mets

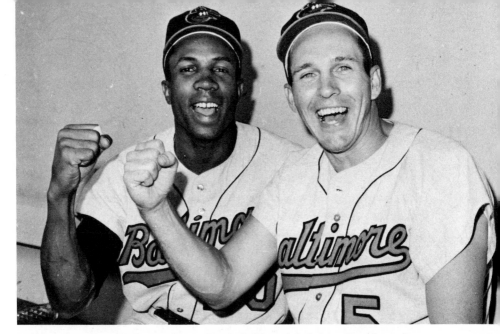

Baltimore's famed Robinson boys, Frank (left) and Brooks, played against the Mets in the '69 Series. Frank was an outfielder; Brooks played third. *Wide World Photos*

had won, 2-1, on a hit by Weis. Met magic had made its first appearance in the Series.

There was no game Monday. The oddsmakers, still unconvinced, made Baltimore a 6-to-5 favorite to win Tuesday's game, and 7-to-5 to win the Series.

These were attractive odds for Met supporters. They were sure that the Mets would come on strong in Shea, where the next three games would be played.

During the August and September pennant drive, the Mets had been almost invincible at home. They had won 25 of the 29 games played in Shea. If they could do that, they ought to take two out of three from Baltimore, and maybe three straight, the Met fans argued.

Another thing in their favor was the way the pitchers had subdued Baltimore's big three hitters in the first two games. Frank Robinson, Boog Powell and Brooks Robinson, batting third, fourth and fifth in the lineup, were the big three. Were they, though? They had collected a total of two singles in 22 at-bats in the two games. This was an ominous sign for the O's, Met fans happily noted.

The first World Series game ever played at Shea Stadium attracted a sell-out crowd of 56,335 despite the threat of rain. The glamour set was there in all its glory—stars of the stage, television and the movies—and other luminaries such as Governor Nelson Rockefeller, Mayor John Lindsay, Jackie Onassis and her two children, and of course, Joan Payson.

Fans who had seen the games in Baltimore commented on the difference between the two cities. In Baltimore in perfect weather, the crowds were well below capacity at both games, and the fans were quiet; in New York the stadium was packed solid and everybody was yelling and having a good time.

The lights went on at one o'clock in cloud-darkened Shea when Gary Gentry started the game by fanning Don Buford. He got Paul Blair to fly out to Tommie Agee in center field. He then walked Frank Robinson, but Boog Powell grounded out to Ken Boswell at second for the third out.

Manager Gil Hodges was a firm believer in the "platoon" system, which meant using left-handed batters against right-handed pitchers, and vice versa. It is supposed to give the batter a slight advantage over the pitcher. He was using his "left-handed lineup" in this game because Jim Palmer, Baltimore's starting pitcher, threw right. It meant benching Weis, Charles, Clendenon and Swoboda.

Tommie Agee, as usual, led off for the Mets. He was one of the club's "double-platoon" men, which meant that he played regularly no matter who was pitching. He was too valuable to bench, as were Cleon Jones, Bud Harrelson and Jerry Grote.

Tommie quickly demonstrated his value to the club by stepping into Palmer's fourth pitch, a fast ball, and knocking it over the wall in center field, 410 feet from home plate. Nothing else happened in that inning. Gary Gentry easily got the O's out in the second, and then the Mets came to bat again.

Palmer retired the first two batters, but walked Jerry Grote. Then Bud Harrelson singled to center. Grote stopped at second. The next batter was Gary Gentry, one of the weakest hitters in the majors. In 74 at-bats during the regular season and the playoffs, he had made only one hit, a double, and had a .081 batting average. At that moment he was 0 for 28. Palmer carelessly threw one over the plate and Gary jumped on it. The ball sailed over Paul Blair's head in shallow center and kept going. Grote and Harrelson scored, Gary got his second hit of the year, and the Mets led, 3-0. This may have been the turning point in the Series.

There was more to come, though. Gary held the Orioles hitless until the fourth, when the big three finally came to life. With one out, Frank Robinson lined a single to left. Then Boog slashed one down the first base line and Frank went to third. Gary whiffed Brooks Robinson. Ellie Hendricks then came up and hit a towering smash to deep left center. Tommie Agee spun right and sprinted after the ball. He made an unbelievable, back-handed, finger-tip catch against the wall at the 396-foot mark. He had saved two runs. The crowd gave him a standing ovation as the trotted to the dugout. They had seen one of the most sensational catches in Series history.

Tommie Agee sprints far to his right to rob Ellis Hendricks of a two-run double in the third game of the Series at Shea. *N.Y. Daily News*

In the eleventh inning of the same game, Agee makes another incredible catch, this time with a belly slide to his left, to kill a rally. *Wide World*

But wait, Tommie wasn't quite yet finished. In the seventh (after the Mets had picked up another run in the sixth) Gary got in trouble again. With two out, he walked Belanger, May and Buford, thus loading the bases. Hodges summoned Nolan Ryan from the bullpen and he took over.

Paul Blair then stepped up to the plate and lined a hard drive to right center. It had "triple" written all over it. Normally, it would have cleared the bases. But Tommie dashed to the edge of the outfield grass and dived when he hit the warning track in front of the fence. Skidding along the ground on his stomach, he kept his glove up and snared the ball. It was an even longer run than he had made before. This time he saved three runs. Counting his first-inning homer, Tommie made a difference of six runs. No outfielder had ever had such a spectacular day in a Series game.

Ed Kranepool hit a homer in the eighth and that was the end of the scoring. The Mets won, 5-0. Gentry was credited with the victory.

Suddenly everything looked rosy for the Mets. They had

Tom Seaver and Jerry Koosman coming up next and they would be playing in good old Shea. How did the oddsmakers feel now?

They felt like changing sides—and did. They made the Mets the favorites at 7 to 5 to win the Series.

Wednesday, October 15, the day of the fourth game, was crisp and cool. Thousands of fans swarmed into Shea before game time to watch batting practice. Not often does a player get cheered in batting practice, but Tommie Agee did. He got an ovation for his deeds in yesterday's game every time he took his turn at bat.

The Mets reverted to the righthanded-batting platoon that Hodges favored against southpaw pitching. Mike Cuellar, the lefty who beat Tom Seaver in the Series opener, would again face him in this game.

It figured to be a pitcher's battle if Tom was in his usual good form—and he was. It was a different Seaver than the one whom the O's had walloped so freely in the opener.

He pitched eight scoreless innings, helped by some great stops by Donn Clendenon. It was, in fact, Clendenon's game most of the way—until the dramatic 10th inning.

Leading off the second inning, Clendenon smashed Cuellar's three-and-two pitch over the left field wall. It was the six-foot -four-inch first baseman's second homer of the Series, and it gave the Mets a 1-0 lead.

First baseman Donn Clendenon gave the Mets their 1-0 lead in the fourth game of the series.

Tom got wobbly in the next inning. Mark Belanger, the first man up, tagged him for a single, and Cuellar followed with another one. Belanger stopped at second.

With the Met infield drawn in at first and third bases for a bunt, Don Buford hit a high, one-hop liner that Clendenon speared back-handed. He rifled the ball to second base for a forceout on Cuellar. Tom then steadied down and retired Paul Blair and Frank Robinson to kill the threat. Donn's glove had saved the day.

The score was still 1-0 when the O's came to bat in the ninth. Paul Blair flied to Swoboda, then Frank Robinson and Boog Powell singled. Frank went to third. Brooks Robinson shot a screamer to right center that looked like a sure hit, but Swoboda dove full length with his gloved hand outstretched and caught the ball. Frank scored after the catch and the game was tied, but Swoboda's daring gamble had kept another run from coming in. A moment later he had to leg it hard to snare Hendricks' long fly to deep right.

The game might explode at any minute, it seemed. It had been a nail-biter since the early innings, and tension mounted in the ninth when Jones and Swoboda singled. But they could not score.

In the top of the 10th, the O's again got two men on, but Tom got out of the jam without damage. He appeared to be tiring, however. Hodges sensed it and decided to take him out if the game went another inning.

Dick Hall came in to pitch for Baltimore in the 10th. Jerry Grote led off with a routine fly to medium short left. Don Buford in left field came in for it but lost the ball in the sun. It fell in front of him for a double. Hodges sent in Rod Gaspar to run for Grote.

Al Weis was purposely passed. The O's were gambling on Seaver batting next and getting him to hit into a double play. But Hodges lifted Tom and put in J. C. Martin to pinch hit. Then the Orioles sent in Pete Richert to pitch.

Martin bunted beautifully. The ball stopped half way to the mound. Both Richert and catcher Ellie Hendricks charged the ball and converged on it. Hendricks yelled for it but Richert snatched it and threw toward first. Rod Gaspar, meanwhile, was tearing for third.

The ball struck Martin on the inside of his left wrist just before he reached first. It caromed off his wrist and dribbled toward second. Rod Gaspar hesitated at third and then, seeing the ball roll free, dashed for the plate and crossed it standing up. The game was over, a 2-1 victory for the Mets.

The next day Shea was bursting at the seams again. The largest crowd yet (57,397) packed the huge steel and concrete structure. From every level of the five-tiered stadium Met fans draped banners of encouragement.

It was another clear, chilly afternoon. "It's my kind of day," said starter Jerry Koosman. The oddsmakers didn't think so, however. They rated Baltimore a 13-10 favorite to win the fifth game, but they refused to take bets on the Series because of the Mets' commanding lead of three games to one.

The day started badly for New York. Dave McNally, the O's starter, walked Tommie Agee, who stole second as Bud Harrelson fanned. Cleon Jones then flied to Frank Robinson in right field and Tommie took third after the catch. Donn Clendenon walked, and the hopeful home fans were on edge as Ron Swoboda came to the plate. But Ron struck out. Disappointment prevailed.

That was nothing, though, compared to how the fans felt in the third inning when the Orioles at last broke out of their batting slump. Mark Belanger opened the inning with a single down the right field line. Then Dave McNally came up, but instead of bunting as pitchers almost always do in a situation like that, he laced a homer into the bullpen in left field. Koosman got the next two batters out but Frank Robinson followed with a bases-empty blast into the left-seats. Boog Powell fanned. The O's led, 3-0. It was the first time since the opening game that they had taken an early lead.

The three-run outburst did not bother Koosman. He weathered the storm and yielded only one more hit the rest of the game. But McNally was also pitching a tight game. In the first five innings he held the Mets at bay and gave them only three scattered hits.

The score was still 3-0 when Cleon Jones led off in the sixth.

McNally threw a low ball that hit Cleon's foot and bounced into the Met dugout. Plate umpire Lou DiMuro called the pitch a ball. Cleon insisted that he had been struck on the instep. Gil Hodges came out of the dugout with the ball and showed the umpire a black smudge of shoe polish on it, thus proving that Cleon's foot had been struck by the ball. Umpire DiMuro changed his call and waved Cleon to first base.

That brought Donn Clendenon to the plate. He whacked a 2-2 pitch to the face of the scoreboard in left field and the Mets trailed by only one run, 3-2. It was Donn's third homer of the Series.

Jerry set the O's down in order in the seventh. Al Weis led off in the Mets' half of the inning. The platooned second baseman had played eight years in the majors both with the Chicago White Sox and the Mets, and had gone to bat more than 600 times before home crowds without hitting a home run. But Al got hold of a fastball from McNally and connected for a homer. He began to run as fast as he could, not knowing that he had done the impossible. "When I got near second base," he later said, "I started hearing the crowd roar and thought something must have happened. I guess I don't know how to react to a home run. I only know how to react to singles and doubles."

The game-tying homer was also Al's fifth Series hit, giving him a .455 average for 11 trips to the plate.

The stage was now set for the Mets to come through and break the 3-3 tie. Eddie Watt was pitching for the O's when Cleon Jones led off in the last of the eighth and smashed a double off the fence in left center. The crowd began rhanting "Let's go, Mets, let's go!" Clendenon then grounded to Brooks Robinson. Cleon stayed on second. Whether to walk Ron Swoboda, the next man up, and try for a double play, or challenge him, was the Oriole's choice. They decided to challenge him. On the second pitch Ron lined a double to left that Buford almost caught at grass level. Cleon came home and the Mets took the lead for the first time, 4-3. Ed Charles flied to Buford for the second out, but the Mets were not yet finished. Jerry Grote ripped a grounder to Boog Powell, but the first baseman bobbled the ball and tossed it to Watt, covering first. Watt, too, bobbled the ball. Swoboda scored all the way from second base with the Mets' fifth run on the two-error play.

All that Jerry Koosman had to do now was to get out three Orioles. He had never been under such pressure as he was at this moment. The crowd sensed it and remained quiet.

A chorus of subdued groans wafted through the stadium as Jerry walked Frank Robinson, the first man up. Then Boog Powell grounded to Al Weis who tossed to Bud Harrelson, covering second, in time to force Frank. One out. Brooks Robinson flied out to Swoboda. Two out, one more to go.

Dave Johnson came up and lifted a long fly to left field. Cleon Jones drifted back, got under it, raised both hands and waited for the ball to drop. *Plop!* It fell into his glove. For a second or two Cleon remained motionless as if to be absolutely sure that he had caught the ball and made the out, and the game was over. Then he dashed for the bullpen to escape the onrushing crowd.

Fans flood the field as their favorites are declared World Champions for 1969.

Gil Hodges and his wife lead the victory parade up Broadway after the Mets won the world championship by defeating the Orioles 4 games to 1. *N.Y. Daily News*

At that moment, 3:14 P.M., Eastern Daylight Time, October 16, 1969, the New York Mets became the baseball champions of the world.

Frantic young fans descended upon the field like an army of paratroopers. They came from all directions and milled about on the field in unrestrained joy, yelling and laughing and grabbing everything in sight, including the players' caps.

Bedlam reigned at the clubhouse celebration. Everybody hugged everybody else. Gil Hodges' face lit up when Casey Stengel embraced him. Mayor Lindsay stood still and grinned while a bottle of champagne was poured on his head. Joan Payson fought back tears, and took a phone call from President Nixon who congratulated her and the team.

The whole city temporarily went out of its mind. People snake-danced in the streets. Total strangers embraced and locked arms. Hundreds of skyscraper windows opened and a deluge of ticker tape and torn paper poured through them—1254 tons of it in all.

Across the nation millions of fans were uplifted by the Mets' miraculous performance. They had done the impossible. They had come from ninth place to the world championship in one year. No other major league team had ever done that, and no other team had ever captured the hearts of the American people, as did the once-lowly Mets, the clowns of baseball.

An estimated 1245 tons of ticker tape and torn paper covered the streets after the celebration. *Wide World Photos*

The New York Times

LATE CITY EDITION

VOL. CXIX....No.40,909

NEW YORK, FRIDAY, OCTOBER 17, 1969

10 CENTS

PRESIDENT IS FIRM ON PUSHING POLICY TO CURB INFLATION

Nixon's Draft Lottery Plan Approved by House Panel

HANOI PROPOSES U.S. AND VIETCONG NEGOTIATE ALONE

Mets Win, 5-3, Take the Series, And a Grateful City Goes Wild

FANS STORM FIELD

Moratorium Backers Say Nixon Will Have to React

The most important news story in 1969 was mankind's giant leap to the moon, according to the *New York Times*—and who would argue about that?

Met fans would, that's who. They said that the Mets' exciting pennant race and the even more exciting World Series triumph was more important than the moon shot, and they had some interesting figures to prove their point. Here they are:

In reporting about the astronauts in 1969, the *New York Times* published pages of photos, charts, diagrams, transcripts of astronaut talk— and 305 stories by *Times* writers.

In reporting about the Mets of 1969, the *Times* published 311 stories by its writers.

Therefore, the score for 1969 was: Mets 311; Moon 305.

The Mets had won again.

MEN WALK ON MOON

ASTRONAUTS LAND ON PLAIN;
COLLECT ROCKS, PLANT FLAG

Voice From Moon: 'Eagle Has Landed'

A Powdery Surface Is Closely Explored

An Analysis of the
Three Miracle Pennant Drives

THE JULY 4 HOLIDAY is a few days short of the exact mid-point of the season and by that time the strongest club in the league has usually asserted itself. More often than not, it is in first place. Thus, the old baseball axiom: the team in first place on July 4 will win the pennant.

Needless to say, it doesn't always work out that way. The tables below show how the miracle teams stood on July 4 and on August 12, when the season was about two-thirds completed.

Club		Games Behind	League Standing	Leading Club
1914 Braves		15	8	Giants
1951 Giants	July 4	8½	2	Dodgers
1969 Mets		5½	2	Cubs
1914 Braves		6½	2	Giants
1951 Giants	August 12	13	2	Dodgers
1969 Mets		9	2	Cubs

Note that between July 4 and August 12 only the Braves had gained ground. They began their last-to-first march in July and by August 12 they were in the middle of a prolonged winning drive.

The other two clubs lost ground after July 4 and on August 12 they appeared to be headed for the depths. Of the two, the Mets were in a better position to make a recovery. They had nine games to make up, with 50 left to play before the season ended. (The Mets played a 162-game season; the other two clubs played the old 154-game schedule.)

The Giants on August 12 faced an almost insurmountable task. They had to gain 13 games on the Dodgers with only 44 left to play. This meant that they had to win 37 games to get a tie—and that is just what they did.

The Giants winning percentage after August 12 was an incredible .840. The figure represents almost nine victories out of every 10 games they played.

Although the Mets did not have as wide a gap to close as the Giants, their winning surge was equally spectacular. The Mets made up their nine-game deficit in less than a month, then went on to finish eight games ahead of the Cubs, for a total gain of 17 games. They won 39 out of their last 50 games and had a winning percentage of .780.

The Braves closed the widest gap of all but they started their drive a month before the other two miracle teams got going. In the cellar on July 4 and 15 games behind the league-leading Giants, they began rolling when they had 76 games left to play. They won 60 and lost 16 for a winning percentage of .789 and finished 10½ games in front of the Giants— a 25½-game climb in all.

What made these teams suddenly come to life and reverse direction? And why did it happen to the Braves in July, and to the Giants and Mets in mid-August?

One can only guess. However, it seems more than a coincidence that all three teams were humiliated and angered by a happening shortly before they began to soar.

Remember the Braves? They were clobbered by a minor-league team and figuratively spat upon by their manager. Humiliated and angered, they were unstoppable thereafter.

Consider the Giants. Crushed by the Dodgers, they sat helpless in their dressing room and listened to the singing taunts of their rivals through the clubhouse walls. Boiling in anger and shame, they responded with a victory march to the summit.

The Mets, too, had their traumatic experience. Seven times in nine games the lowly Astros had defeated them, and when they faced each other in the final series of the season, the revenge-seeking Mets were destroyed in three straight games. It was enough to make a club quit, but the Mets rallied, took 12 of the next 13 games, and never stopped running forward.

Of course, many a team that has suffered humiliation has collapsed in helpless anger, but the miracle teams were made of sterner stuff. They possessed that hard-to-define quality called spirit. The word comes from the Latin *spirare* which means to breathe, to be alive, to have courage, vivacity and enthusiastic loyalty.

The miracle teams had all those qualities and more. In addition, they had good managers and good pitching—the essentials for a winner. They were not great teams; there wasn't a star or a superstar among them, but they were good. What is more important, they knew they were good enough to win and nothing could stop them. Call it spirit. They had it.

HOMERIC HOMERS

Bobby Thomson's pennant-winning homer had hardly stopped bouncing before the baseball writers were at their typewriters hammering out columns about it. His was a healthy blow, by no means a cheap homer just out of reach near the foul line. It landed far up in the left field seats and would have probably dropped at about 375 feet from the plate in an open field.

It could not have been caught in any baseball park in the majors then or now. The longest left field in the majors today is 355 feet (home plate to left field at the foul line) in Wrigley Feld, Chicago, the home of the Cubs. The shortest is 309 feet, in the Orioles' Memorial Stadium, Baltimore. The average distance is about 330 feet to both left and right fields. To center field the average is 410 feet.

John Franklin Baker was the first slugger of this century to blast his way to fame by hitting homers when they counted most. He played third for the Philadelphia A's in 1911 when they faced the Giants in the World Series.

Thanks to Baker's timely homers, the A's won four games to two. Baker, who threw right handed and batted left, became a national figure. He was known throughout the land as "Home Run" Baker. He led the American League in homers four years in a row, hitting 9 in 1911, 10 in 1912, 12 in 1913 and 8 in 1914, for a total of 39 homers.

These days a lot of players hit that many in one season—but don't laugh. Home Run Baker was hitting the "dead" ball, which was usually stained black with tobacco juice. He swung a thick-handled, unwieldy bat against spitballs, shiners and emery balls—trick deliveries long since outlawed. No wonder a home run was a rarity in those days.

One of the most talked-about homers was Babe Ruth's wallop in the fifth inning of the third game in the 1932 World Series when the Yankees were playing the Cubs in Chicago. The Yankees had won the first two games in New York.

The score was tied, 4-4, in the fifth when the Babe, who had hit a homer in the first inning, came to bat again. The crowd had been riding him hard all during the game and now they were heckling him more than ever.

Charlie Root, the Cubs' pitcher, fed him a strike. The Babe took it and then defiantly pointed to the most distant part of Wrigley Field. The gesture was clear. He was showing the world just where he was going to put his next homer. The crowd booed more than ever. Babe let another strike go by. Again he pointed to deep center field, and again the crowd hooted.

Charlie Root sent the third one across the plate and this time Ruth went for it. He connected squarely. The ball streaked over the outfield like a projectile and landed in the center field bleachers. The Babe had called his shot perfectly. He laughed so hard as he circled the bases that he could hardly find the bags.

Later, Charlie Root said that Ruth was simply holding up his fingers to show the number of strikes, and some sports writers agreed with him. However, most of the scribes who saw the game said that the Babe really did point to the bleachers and call his shot. Umpire George Magerkurth, who was behind the plate, agreed with them, as did Lou Gehrig, Ruth's teammate. And the Babe himself always said he pointed. In any event, it was the most dramatic homer the Babe ever hit.

The "Homer in the Gloaming" is the name of one of baseball's most famous home runs, so called because it was hit in the semi-darkness of a lightless ball park with a pennant at stake.

It was struck on September 28, 1938, three days before the end of the season, in a game between the Pirates and the Cubs in Wrigley Field. The Pirates were leading the league with a scant half-game margin over the Cubs. Dark clouds hung over the park as the game developed into a seesaw struggle. Pittsburg led in the eighth inning, 5-3, but the Cubs rallied in their half and put across two runs. At the start of the ninth darkness was falling fast.

The umpires went into a huddle. Should they end the game and call it a 5-5 tie? This would force the clubs to play a doubleheader the next day. It was really getting dark, but they decided to try for a full nine innings.

Charlie Root got the Pirates out quickly. Then Mace Brown, a relief pitcher for Pittsburg, worked fast and retired the first two Cub batters. The next man up was catcher Gabby Hartnett, the Cubs' playing manager, who was then 38 years old and past his peak. He was a long-ball hitter and still dangerous.

The darkness favored a fast ball, but Mace Brown used his best pitch, a curve. Gabby swung at it and missed. Again Mace threw a curve and this time Gabby got a piece of it and fouled it back. The crowd groaned.

With two out and two strikes on Gabby, Mace tried for a waste pitch, low and outside, but the ball slipped over the plate. Gabby leaned into it. Before he had taken two steps toward first, he knew it was going into the stands.

Gabby's "Homer in the Gloaming" put the Cubs in first place by half a game. And it took the fight out of the Pirates. The next day the Cubs slaughtered them, 10-1, and the following day they clinched the flag.

After the Cubs' gallant finish in the pennant race, fans all over the country were pulling for them to take the Series, but the powerful Yankees again humiliated them by winning four straight.

There came a day of reckoning for the unbeatable Yankees, however. A timely homer brought them down.

It happened in Pittsburg on October 13, 1960. The Yankees and the Pirates were tied at three games apiece in the World Series and were about to play the seventh and final game. The New Yorkers were heavily favored to take the big one, for only the day before they had demolished the Pirates with a 17-hit bombardment, and had won, 12 to 0. It was the biggest shutout margin in Series history.

It was 9-9 when Bill Mazeroski, the first man up for the Pirates, strode to the plate in the bottom of the ninth. The 24-year-old second baseman was not considered a dangerous hitter. His season's average was .273 and he was down in the eighth spot in the Pittsburg batting order.

Yankee pitcher Ralph Terry offered Maz a low curve. It was a ball. Then Terry released his high fast one. Maz swung at it. *Boom!* Delirious fans in the left field seats scrambled for the ball as it came down.

Waving his helmet at each step and hopping up and down as he ran, Maz fought his way from third to home through a mass of back-slappers and scored the run that gave the Pirates the World Championship. It was the most dramatic homer since Bobby Thomson's famed shot nine years before.

The question of who hit the longest home run will never be answered with certainty because this is one phase of baseball on which no official records have been kept. Any home run that travels 450 feet or more would clear the deepest center field in the majors (Detroit's Tiger Stadium, 440 feet) and would be classified as a "tape-measure" homer by collectors of baseball memorabilia. The term means a giant homer, one that deserves measurement with a tape.

There have been many drives that went from 450 to 500 feet on the fly and several have topped the 500-foot mark in major league competition. Only a very few have carried over 550 feet.

Babe Ruth hit a number of "tape-measure" drives that came to earth well past the 500-foot mark, but only one of them was actually measured. He hit it in the spring of 1919 in an exhibition game with the Giants in Tampa, Florida. It was 586 feet.

Ruth hit a mighty homer in a regular game in Detroit that may have been the daddy of them all. He socked it off Ken Holloway on June 8, 1926. The ball cleared the right center field stands and bounded into the street a block away. The crowd and the reporters in the press box sat open-mouthed as the ball disappeared from sight. The colossal clout was never measured, but New York and Detroit baseball writers at the game estimated that it carried at least 600 feet.

One of the most difficult feats a player can achieve is to hit 50 or more home runs in one season. Only nine players in this century have been able to do it. It is a feat almost as rare as the unassisted triple play, which has been executed only eight times in major league baseball.

As a measure of its rarity, consider the great sluggers who did *not* hit 50 homers in one year: Hank Aaron, Ted Williams, Joe DiMaggio, Harmon Killebrew, Willie Stargell and Frank Robinson, to name a few.

Lou Gehrig back in the 1930's twice hit 49, as did Killebrew in the 1960's, but they failed to make the magic number. Four of the nine players who made the grade, did it twice. They are: Jimmy Foxx, Ralph Kiner, Mickey Mantle and Willie Mays. Babe Ruth, the one and only, achieved the feat four times (in 1920, '21, '27 and '28).

Mickey Mantle might have had several 50-homer years had he not been hampered by a series of injuries and ailments. The 195-pound, broad-backed Mantle wound up his career in 1968 with a total of 536 homers, which put him among the first 10 all-time home-run champions. He hit from either side of the plate. It made no difference to the Mick. He hit the ball out of sight often enough to lead the league in homers four times. Several of his blasts were in the tape-measure class; they went deep into all three fields.

Mantle and his long-ball hitting teammate Roger Maris, gripped the nation's baseball fans from coast to coast in 1961 with their assault on Babe Ruth's home run record (60 in 1927), and their duel with each other. Maris batted third in the lineup, Mantle fourth, and from the start of the season the M & M boys, as they were called, began walloping homers with great frequency. It soon became a home run race between the two blond outfielders.

Daily the nation's sports pages gave full coverage to the battle, and almost daily the M & M boys had to endure tedious press interviews. One question the press continually asked was whether Ruth's mark could be broken that season under the new and longer 162-game schedule. (The American League expanded from eight to 10 clubs in 1961 and for the first time played eight more games than the clubs previously did under the traditional 154-game season.) Clearly, the M & M boys would have an eight-game advantage over the Babe.

In early September when Ruth's record seemed in jeopardy, Baseball Commissioner Ford Frick announced that he would not consider the Babe's mark broken unless the feat were achieved in 154 games.

By this time the strain on the home-run twins was beginning to show. Maris' hair fell out in one spot on his head. His doctor told him it was caused by "nerves." Mickey was short tempered with reporters and tried to hide from them. Through it all both players remained good friends. In fact, they shared an apartment together—at a secret address where the press could not find them.

Late in September an ailing, exhausted Mantle could go on no longer. He withdrew on September 19. He had hit 54 homers, his most ever.

The crew-cut Maris, whose batting average was only .269, now had the race to himself. On September 20 in the team's 154th game he belted his 59th homer—one short of Ruth's mark in the same number of team games.

Ruth's record was now safe, according to the Commissioner's pronouncement, and most fans agreed, especially oldtimers who winced at the thought of the unpopular Maris toppling the Babe from his throne. However, Maris' admirers argued that no matter what the Commissioner had decreed, Ruth's mark would be tied or broken if Maris continued to hit homers in the eight extra games ahead of him. A season is a season, they argued.

Maris drew crowds everywhere he played. About half of the fans came to see him fail. Groans and cheers filled the air in Yankee Stadium in the third inning of Game Number 159 on September 26, when Maris got his 60th homer, off Baltimore's Jack Fisher (10-13).

On October 1, the last day of the season, Maris blasted his 61st homer off Tracey Stallard, a Red Sox rookie with a 2-7 record. It was Game Number 162.

It must be rated a Homeric homer, for Maris had truly hit more home runs in an official major league season than had ever been hit by anyone else. But did he really break Ruth's record? The answer seems to be yes and no. The record books present only the statistics:

Most home runs, season

61 Roger Maris, A.L., N.Y. 1961 (162-game season)
60 Babe Ruth, A.L., N.Y. 1927 (154-game season)

It must be remembered that Maris had a lot of things in his favor in 1961 besides the longer season (actually, he played in 10 more games that year then Ruth did in 1927). Maris faced a greater number of inferior pitchers—castoffs from the original eight clubs, and rookies from the minors brought up to stock the two new teams. He had the benefit of the new strike zone, which was purposely reduced in size by the rulesmakers to give the batter an advantage over the pitcher and thus increase run production. The plan worked, aided by the new whiplash (thin-handled) bat and jackrabbit ball.

In 1927 the American League clubs hit a total of 439 home runs; in 1961 those eight clubs collected 1226 homers—almost three times the number hit in Ruth's day. (The eight-club National League produced about the same ratio in homers—from 483 to 1196 in the same span of years. The fact that home run production had almost tripled since Ruth's time, did not mean that the hitters were three times better than those of the 1920's. It meant, rather, that it was three times easier to hit a homer than it had been in the old days.

On March 13, 1954, Bobby Thomson, who had been traded to the Milwaukee Braves, fractured an ankle in a spring training game in Florida. The event was duly reported in the press, along with mention of Bobby's big homer in the Polo Grounds three years before.

Scarcely mentioned, if at all, was the name of the player who replaced Bobby in the game. He was a 20-year-old softspoken rookie from Mobile, Alabama. His name was Henry Louis Aaron.

Thus began the career of one of the all-time "greats" who would one day conquer the Mount Everest of sports achievement—Babe Ruth's 714 home runs. It was the one Ruthian record that was supposedly unassailable. Many believed that it would stand forever, including the Babe himself, who said so many times.

It took Hank 21 years to scale the heights and most of that time he trod the quiet road, playing superb ball year after year with great consistency and without fanfare.

He was a neglected hero during most of his career. Not until he was within striking distance of Ruth's record did he get his long-deserved recognition from the fans and writers. The players recognized his talents from the start, though, especially the league's pitchers. They called him "Bad Henry." It was a compliment.

"Throwing a fastball by Bad Henry," said Cardinal pitcher Curt Simmons, "is like trying to sneak the sun past a rooster."

A natural hitter, the slight right-hander stood far back in the batter's box and got his power from his thick, whippy wrists. They measured eight inches around. In his 21 years with the Braves (Milwaukee and Atlanta, 1954-74), he never had a bad year. He consistently hit .300 or better, averaged more than 35 homers a season, led the league in RBIs four times, in total bases eight times, played first base and center field with equal grace and effectiveness (he won three Gold Glove Awards).

For all that, Hank played in the shadow of Wondrous Willie Mays most of the time. Willie was a more exciting player, more colorful and magnetic than the plodding Aaron, and he got the headlines. He deserved them, too. In his prime Willie surpassed Hank in many categories—stolen bases, home runs, batting average and RBIs.

There was much talk in baseball circles about the possibility of one or the other upsetting Ruth's mark, possibly both if Willie could keep up the pace. He was three years older than Hank.

Willie's peak year was 1965 when he walloped 52 homers and raced the 500 mark. Aaron reached his 500 mark in 1958. He hit 44 homers in 1969, 38 the next year and 47 in 1971, his best year.

Mays had slowed down to a walk by this time. He hit only 18 in 1971, but he still had a paper-thin margin over Hank in total homers, 646 to 639.

The race was about over. This saddened many of Willie's admirers. They knew that the Giant superstar had lost almost two full seasons to the Army at the ages of 21 and 22. It had cost him a probable 62 homers, they said, based on his performance the year before he left for service, and the first year he returned. Adding those 62 to his total would have given him 708, enough to break Ruth's 714 mark in 1972.

It was obvious that Hank would soon catch up with his friendly rival—and he did on May 31, 1972, when he belted his 648th homer in the first inning of Atlanta's game against San Diego. He was now tied with Willie for second place on the all-time home run list. Both stayed at 648 for a few days, then Hank drew away and finished out of sight. He got 34 homers for a total of 673.

At last national attention came to "the little slugger of the Braves," as a *New York Times* reporter described the six-foot athlete. Hank became the nation's sports hero, the most celebrated, talked-about baseball player since the Ruthian era.

At the start of the 1973 season Hank was 41 homers short of tying the Babe. All through the summer of 1973 the nation's eyes were on him. He was having a good season and it was just possible that he might reach the magic numbers before it ended. The two historic clouts, Numbers 714 and 715, became the most discussed and written-about home runs in history long *before* they were hit.

Hank almost made it in 1973. He slugged a surprising 40 homers for a total of 713 and had just one to go when the 1974 season opened. He was then 40 but just as trim and lithe as he was when he took over Bobby Thomson's job.

In spring training that year, the Braves' owner William Bartholomay, announced that Aaron would be benched during the club's opening series in Cincinnati (April 4, 5, 6) so that Atlanta fans could have a chance to see him hit the historic blows at home and thus jack up attendance. The press was outraged, and so were a multitude of fans. Baseball Commissioner Bowie Kuhn ended the uproar by ordering the Braves to play Aaron in at least two of the three opening games—and that was that.

On Thursday night, April 4, in Cincinnati, Aaron stepped to the plate and on his first swing of the season blasted a 380-footer into the left field seats. It gave the Braves a 3-0 first-inning lead, and gave Hank a tie with Babe Ruth at Number 714.

The game was halted for six minutes for ceremonies. Vice President Gerald Ford told Aaron on the field: "This is a great day for baseball and for you. Good luck for 715."

Hank sat out the next game, but played on Sunday in Cincinnati and went hitless in three listless appearances. On to Atlanta went the Braves to face the Los Angeles Dodgers.

On the evening of April 8 before a jam-packed Atlanta crowd of 53,775 and a national television audience, Hank came to bat in the first inning against left-hander Al Downing. Al walked him amid boos from every corner of the stadium.

In the fourth inning Hank faced Downing again, this time with teammate Darrell Evans on base. Hank took a ball and got set for the next pitch. Downing let it go at exactly 9:07. *Crack!* The ball shot over the left-center fence.

For the first time in his career Hank stopped on the base path to first to watch his homer go all the way. It was the most Homeric of all homers. The fans of the nation must have thought so, too. Within the next few hours Hank received 20,000 telegrams—more•than any sports hero ever received on any single occasion, according to Western Union.

Fewer than 6,000 people were in Atlanta Stadium to see Homer Number 716. Hank finished the 1974 season with a total of 733 home runs, then said good-bye to the Braves. He left them as the most honored played of his time.

Selected Bibliography

MUCH OF THE MATERIAL in this book came from the author's sports library, which contains more than 100 hard-cover baseball books, the complete issues of *Sport* and *Sports Illustrated* since those magazines began publication, and uncountable thousands of clippings from various periodicals and newspapers going back to the turn of the century.

Also included is the mammoth (2,337 pages) and indispensable *Baseball Encyclopedia*, first published by Macmillan in 1969; and the *Encyclopedia of Baseball* (745 pages), published by A. S. Barnes, 1971.

Most of the annual record books in the library are published by the *Sporting News* of St. Louis, a widely-read weekly devoted to sports, which is almost as old as baseball itself. The *Baseball Register*, the *Baseball Guide*, the *Baseball Record Book* and the *World Series Records* are published annually by the *Sporting News*. These soft-cover books are accurate, complete and inexpensive. The *News* also publishes from time to time *Daguerreotypes of Great Stars of Baseball*, which contains the lifetime records of more than 365 stars of the past.

I am particularly grateful to Clifford Kachline, Historian of the National Baseball Library in Cooperstown for his help in the preparation of this book, and to Joan Payson, an old friend who created the Mets and in so doing made this book possible.

A grateful nod also to Leonard Koppett for his excellent book, *The New York Mets*, to Roger Kahn for his fine article, *The Day Bobby Hit the Home Run* (*Sports Illustrated*, Oct. 10, 1960), to Willie Mays who co-authored *I Came to Play* (*True*, May, 1955), and to Jack Newcombe for his *Bobby Thomson, the Unwilling Hero* (*Sport*, May, 1955).

The following titles represent a partial list of those I used in researching this book:

Allen, Lee. *The World Series*. New York: Putnam, 1969.
Brandt, Bill. *Do You Know Your Baseball?* New Jersey: Barnes, 1947.
Breslin, Jimmy. *Can't Anybody Here Play This Game?* New York: Viking, 1963.

Broeg, Bob. *Superstars of Baseball. The Sporting News,* 1971.

Buchanan, Lamont. *The World Series.* New York: Dutton, 1951.

Danzig, A., and Brandwein, P. Editors. *The Greatest Sports Stories From The New York Times.* New Jersey: Barnes, 1951.

Durant, John. *The Story of Baseball.* New York: Hastings House, 1973.

———. *Highlights of the World Series.* New York: Hastings House, 1973.

Fitzgerald, Ed. *The American League.* New Jersey: Barnes, 1952.

———. *The National League.* New Jersey: Barnes, 1952.

Grayson, Harry. *They Played the Game.* New Jersey: Barnes, 1944.

Koppett, Leonard. *The New York Mets.* New York: Macmillan, 1970.

Krueger, Joseph J. *Baseball's Greatest Drama.* Kreuger, 1946.

Libby, Bill. *Star Pitchers of the Major Leagues.* New York: Random, 1971.

Lieb, Frederick G. *The Story of the World Series.* New York: Putnam, 1949.

———. *The Baseball Story.* New York: Putnam, 1950.

Meany, Tom. *Baseball's Greatest Teams.* New Jersey: Barnes, 1949.

———. *Baseball's Greatest Hitters.* New Jersey: Barnes, 1950.

———. *Baseball's Greatest Pitchers.* New Jersey: Barnes, 1951.

———. *Baseball's Greatest Players.* New York: Dell, 1955.

———. *The Incredible Giants.* New Jersey: Barnes, 1955.

Pope, Edwin. *Baseball's Greatest Managers.* New York: Doubleday, 1960.

Schiffer, Don, ed. *My Greatest Baseball Game.* New Jersey: Barnes, 1950.

Smith, Ira. *Baseball's Famous Pitchers.* New Jersey: Barnes, 1954.

———. *Baseball's Famous Outfielders.* New Jersey: Barnes, 1954.

Smith, Robert. *Baseball's Hall of Fame.* New York: Bantam, 1973.

———. *Baseball.* New York: Simon & Schuster, 1957.

Seaver, Tom (with Dick Schaap). *Tom Seaver and the Mets.* New York: Dutton, 1970.

Siwoff, Seymour, ed. *The Book of Baseball Records.* Siwoff, 1972.

Walsh, Christie. *Baseball's Greatest Lineup.* New Jersey: Barnes, 1952.

Ward, Arch. *The Greatest Sports Stories From The Chicago Tribune.* New Jersey: Barnes, 1953.

Index

156

159